The Federal Reserve System
"In God We Trust"

By Rasheed L. Muhammad
RLM Publishing

Second Revised Edition 2010

This book is dedicated to the
Native Americans

Acknowledgements: Thanks to God (Allah), his divine messengers and servants. Thanks to the freest black man on earth, Minister Louis Farrakhan, for dealing with the subject concerning the Federal Reserve System to Black America, the most unaware people on the U.S. scene and its state of affairs. A Special thanks to Bro. Victor Muhammad of Mosque 11, Boston Mass for suggesting this new book cover design.

Table of Content

Introduction

The Federal Reserve System "In God We Trust" you shall read how powerful paper money has become over the lives of most modern world inhabitants. Although many people profess to trust in God, by whatever name he is called, paper money is sought after far above the ordinances of God. Some people even silently pray to God for money so they can buy what their hearts desire. Men and women, by nature, pursue goods and services with tendencies to want what our neighbors own because ownership ties directly to ones purchase power and self-esteem.

In America the motto, "IN GOD WE TRUST" was placed on coins during the 18th century. Although Blacks were held as slaves, white Americans made many appeals to Secretary of the Treasury Salmon P. Chase to include a Deity name on U.S. coins to pronounce their devoutness to God and the sovereignty of America and its national affairs. As a result, Secretary Chase instructed James Pollock, Director of the Mint at Philadelphia, to prepare a motto, in a letter dated November 20, 1861:

Dear Sir: No nation can be strong except in the strength of God, or safe except in His defense. The trust of our people in God should be declared on our national coins.

You will cause a device to be prepared without unnecessary delay with a motto expressing in the fewest and tersest words possible this national recognition.

Ninety-five years later, on July 30, 1956, President Dwight D. Eisenhower signed a law declaring "*In God We Trust*" the official motto of the United States. Below is a listing by denomination of the first production and delivery dates for currency bearing IN GOD WE TRUST:[1]

DENOMINATION	*PRODUCTION*	*DELIVERY*
$1 Federal Reserve Note	February 12, 1964	March 11, 1964
$5 United States Note	January 23, 1964	March 2, 1964
$5 Federal Reserve Note	July 31, 1964	September 16, 1964
$10 Federal Reserve Note	February 24, 1964	April 24, 1964
$20 Federal Reserve Note	October 7, 1964	October 7, 1964
$50 Federal Reserve Note	August 24, 1966	September 28, 1966
$100 Federal Reserve Note	August 18, 1966	September 27, 1966

Over all people, do not care who prints money and how it affects their daily lives. As

---

[1] http://www.ustreas.gov/education/fact-sheets/currency/in-god-we-trust.shtml

long as money can be spent on food, clothing, houses, furniture, fuel, medicine, education, sport and play nothing else matters. Money is looked upon as wealth. It is what supports or embellishes our immediate surroundings and needs.

In antiquity, the best comforts and needs were mainly reserved for royal family members, their inner court executives and government officials whom all grew to feel a sense of entitlement and privilege due their nearness to royals. Whether they were ancient Egyptians, Hindus, Greeks, Romans, Africans or Arabs royalty is royalty and the privileges thereof have not changed today.

Antiquity demonstrates if you were born into wealth (wealthy circles or families with superior qualities), you are entitled to the best comforts known to man. On the other hand, if you were born into an agricultural or low-income family then luxury items and the lifestyle of the "rich and famous" too often remained unreachable.

Throughout the ages, due to dissatisfaction of the masses, a new monetary policy was borne out of 16th century medieval Europe. The merchant class of business came to understand the sciences, which dealt with man in his business relations and how business matters tie directly to a *fiat-money*[2] median of exchange or credit system. That is to advance wealth before it is earned.

Wealth is the general economic term used to include all things that satisfy human wants or which, as the economists say, have the quality of utility whereby anyone can purchase whatever their hearts desire. So this, the poor masses have always desired secretly in their hearts. Millions of human beings have always kept a watchful eye and desire for items and trinkets that wealth represents but could not readily afford to pay the cost. Therefore, "*get it now and pay later*" was not difficult to advertise. Hence, the Latin term *fiat* meaning, "let it be done" became an ecomonic tool for the modern conveniences many enjoy and desire.

Under modernity's current monetary system of the West; designed to temporarily satisfy the desires of the dissatisfied who yearn for comfort and symbols of wealth, the general public did not realize and do not understand what it would cost surrendering individual and national sovereignty in

---

[2] The term derives from the Latin *fiat*, meaning "let it be done". Where fiat money is used as currency, the term **fiat currency** is used. Today, most national currencies are fiat currencies, including the US dollar, the euro, and all other reserve currencies.

exchange to spend credit or fiat money for goods, services and luxury items.

Fact is those who mismanaged this world's monetary policy continue to operate on a trial and error bases. While fiscal policy developed largely from academic theory, the development of monetary policy has been heavily influenced by the trial-and-error experience of policymakers.[3] Therefore, U.S. credit or fiat money is an experimental piece of paper called "Federal Reserve Notes." It was designed to initially afford everyone enough purchase power for homes, fine clothes, shoes, diamonds, gold rings, education, comfort and whatever else one may conceive. The long-term problem, however, is that the Federal Reserve Note also carries with it a perpetual debt for the recipients who employ it. That debt also applies to the U.S. government as well.

The people living in the United States of America symbolize a nation of debtors more than any other commercial nation on earth. Why is this so? Firstly, *fiat money* was phased into America's economy during the 1930's. By this I mean, Europe's international bank cartels combined and trusted themselves to regulate prices and output of printing money for the new world—North

[3] http://ingrimayne.com/econ/monetaryhistory/Overview15A.html

America, as a rule, specifically in 1913, December 23.

What you shall discover in this book is when the founding fathers of the 13 colonies were sent to America, Europe's elitists never meant for them to conduct business outside of England's 16th century bank structure. Thus, a plan was hatched to capture the U.S. market by controlling its monetary policy and currency production.

Although the U.S. modern Federal Reserve System is simultaneously a curse and a blessing because it means you must go into debt to employ its credit and fiat money, the Federal Reserves response to the secret desires of the poor and dissatisfied on hard times and with little access to immediate purchase power did present immediate gratification. In fact, it gave (1) hope to people who yearned to become *big spenders* and feel equal to the wealthy and (2) made the U.S. government a welfare state under *The **Federal Reserve Act** (ch. 6, 38 Stat. 251, enacted December 23, 1913, 12 U.S.C. ch.3)*. In summary, consumer slavery of all people, it was discovered more profitable than chattel slavery.

Rasheed L. Muhammad
01/13/2010

Chapter I

U.S. For Sale

So-called faithful and true American Christians could not master the science of economics as presented within their book of scripture. Therefore, business proponents of Europe's 16th Talmudic-merchant Jewish banking establishment acquired control of the embryonic U.S. treasury between 1913 and 1933. They had very little regard to what the Biblical or Quranic God mentions about usurious lending practices.

> 24. *"When you lend money to any of My people, to the poor among you, you shall not be to him as a creditor, nor shall you impose upon him any interest. If you take your neighbor's [night] garment as a pledge (collateral), you shall return it to him by nightfall." (Exodus 22: 24 – 26)*
>
> 37. *"You shall not lend him your money for usury, nor lend him your food at a profit." (Leviticus 25:35-37)*
>
> 5. *"He who does not put out his money at usury, Nor does he take a bribe against the innocent. He who does these things shall never be moved." (Psalm 15:5)*
>
> 12. *"In you they take bribes to shed blood; you take usury and increase; you have made profit from your neighbors by extortion, and have forgotten Me," says the Lord GOD." (Ezekiel 22:12)*

To circumvent usury prohibitions, medieval aristicrats and kings and merchants and bank cartels of Europe discovered a way to justify excess usury. In spite of the Old Testament prohibitions against its practice, an ancient writing was employed from Babylon to justify excess usury.

Talmudic Monetary Policy

The *Talmud* or Babylonian Talmud is the collection of ancient Jewish laws, which governs the religious and non-religious life of European Jews of these modern times. Under Talmudic law, charging interest (riba) on loans is permissible.

> The Pharisaical system of "Commercial Law", as codified in the "*Babylonian Talmud*"; was at that time Forcibly Imposed by the Romanistic-Normans over the previously Non-Romanized Christian/Common-Law Saxon-Anglo/English People. This is shown as follows:
>
> ***"The Jews, whom the Normans brought to England . . . [or who financed and followed the invasion - Ed.] brought a refined system of commercial law: their own form of commerce and a system of rules to facilitate and govern it... Several elements of historical Jewish legal practice have been integrated into the English legal system. Notable among these is the written credit agreement - shetar, or starr, as it appears in English documents. The basis of the shetar,***

starr or "Jewish Gage," was a lien on all property (including realty) that has been traced as a source of the modern mortgage. Under Jewish law, the shetar permitted a creditor to proceed against all the goods and land of the defaulting debtor...

Jewish law that debts could be recovered against a loan secured by "all property, movable and immovable" was a weapon of socio-economic change that tore the fabric of feudal society and established the power of liquid wealth in place of land holding...Jewish Law, wherein personal debt superseded rights in real property had become the law of the land." "Footnote 11: H.C. Richardson, The English Jewry Under Angevin Kings *94 (1960)*

Jews liquidation of land obligations broke down rigidity of feudal land tenure and facilitated transfer of land to new capitalist class). Footnote 15: CF. 1 F. Pollock and F.W. Maitland, supra note 3 at 469... (alien to English law for creditor not in possession of land to have rights in it)."[4]

Essentially, Babylonian Talmudic law is rooted in Master/Slave relationships. It is designed wherein someone must be in debt to another. Debt is the consequence of excess usury. This practice is in total violation to Allah (God)—Original Black Nation of Asia's divine economic law.

---

[4] www.biblebelievers.org.au/babelaw.htm

The unique Quranic word used for usury was riba, which literally means “excess or addition”. A perfect example of usury in the Christian world is pay-loan enterprises found mostly in low-income business districts. Sometimes pay loan interest rates are as high as 600%. These pay loan operations actually began in Italy by Lombard pawnshop lenders. The Islamic world of business forbids such lending abuses.

All commercialized governments and people need loans from time to time. Ideally in the Islamic world, finance is used for potential commercially profitable activity. Both the provider (banker or lender) and borrower bear the risk of possible loss. There is no guarantee for the principal and no guarantee for the return. Moreover, there is nothing to prohibit the government from printing money. It has but to take care that the benefits outweigh the costs.[5]

Who Owns US Bonds

The Bureau of the Public Debt is an agency within the Fiscal Service of the United States Treasury Department. Under authority derived from “Article I, section 8 of the Constitution, Public Debt is responsible for borrowing the money

[5] http://www.ifew.com/insight/13036mon/bkreview.htm

needed to operate the federal government. So far U.S. Treasury Bonds have not failed. The United States government debt, commonly called the "public debt" or the "national debt", is the amount of money owed by the Federal government of the United States to holders of U.S. debt instruments.

"While the public debt of the United States can be traced to the beginning of the nation itself in 1776, Public Debt, as it's known today, was officially created in 1940. The creation was part of a Treasury reorganization plan where the Public Debt Service was officially designated the Bureau of the Public Debt...

"The Wholesale Securities Services program contributes to Treasury's priority of financing the debt at the lowest cost over time by guaranteeing operational readiness to meet the government's financing needs and protecting and strengthening Treasury's borrowing capabilities. It also educates and builds relationships with large investors and preserves confidence in Treasury auctions through the auction rule compliance program."[6]

We are now in a trillion trillions of dollar debt to the bourgeoisie of a new international world order. Wealthy private individuals, families, corporations, central banks and various funds worldwide own a

6 http://en.wikipedia.org/wiki/Bureau_of_the_Public_Debt#Mission_and_Vision

piece of the U.S. economy by purchasing treasury bonds.

Up to now, our Bureau of the Public Debt, for what it is worth, has failed every U.S. citizen. (See chart below)

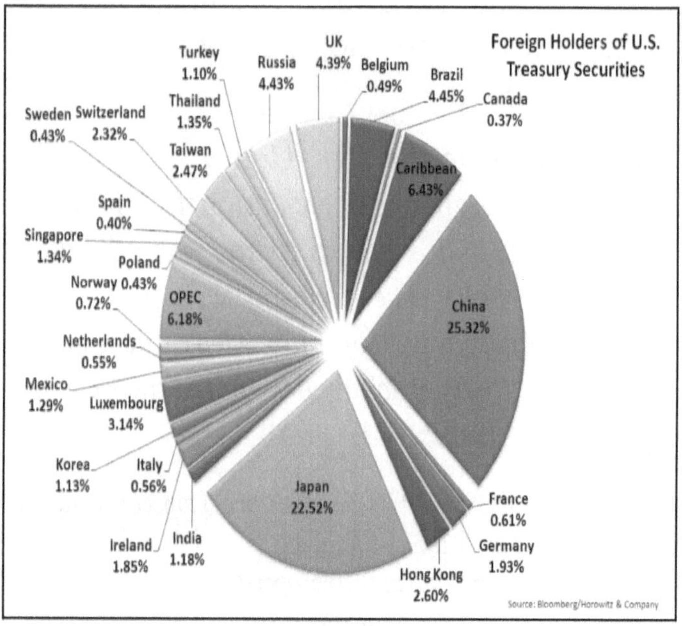

Essentially, selling bonds represent the debasement or weakening of U.S. purchase power (wealth) because bonds possess usurious interest rates. This practice was legalized during 16th century England to assure that private investors among Europe's Gentile aristicratic and Jewish merchant class receive a return on investments. Particuarly in the form of loans made for commerce and trade adventures by land and sea.

Today since the federal US government continues to be financed by usurious loans to function and exist and raises funds (by selling Treasury bills, notes, bonds, U.S. Savings Bonds, etc) under outdated finance rules and regulations of ancient Babylon, America is on course toward self-destruction.

Unfortunately, the U.S. Government House of Representatives, Congress and Senators have fulfilled the role of the biblical harlot for selling out its citizenry to usury barons. Without consistently regulating the practice of usury, U.S. debt as of 2010 now stands around 14 trillion dollars and rising.

Many U.S. citizens do not realize how or why they were put in bondage under *The*

***Federal Reserve Act** (ch. 6, 38 Stat. 251, enacted December 23, 1913, 12 U.S.C. ch.3)*. Simply, U.S. Congress under President Woodrow Wilson and the U.S. Senate, on December 23, 1913, agreed to the "Act" by a vote of 43 yeas to 25 nays with 27 not voting. This particular "Act" prepostioned every women, man and child in a type of bondage in which Allah (God) and the Holy Quran absolutely oppose!

Under the Federal Reserve Act, our income taxes were *legally* swindled under the color of law with the establishment of the Federal Reserve System. And by so doing, Europe's 16th century Central Banking apparatus establishment were guaranteed a return on their U.S. investment during the 1930's onward. Were the Federal Reserve Act not passed, no foreign lender/investor would be guaranteed to receive a return on US Treasury Bonds as promised from pre-appropriated US income taxes.

When an entity buys a U.S. T-bond, they are lending money to prolong U.S. government operations by excess usury. Therefore, nowadays the dollar is not worth the paper it is printed. Furthermore, the value of America's gold supply does not even collateralize the Federal Reserve Note to justify more borrowing to payoff U.S. debt. This only means an economic collapse is imminent.

Greek history makes this very clear. Selling your citizens to payoff foreign debt never succeeds for long.

"**800-600 B.C.** *Both Plato and Aristotle believed usury was immoral and unjust. The Greeks at first regulate interest, and then deregulate it. After deregulation, there* *was so much unregulated debt that Athenians were sold into slavery and threatened revolt."*[7]

Of course, the U.S. government has never defaulted on its U.S. T-Bonds. Some bankers profess, "as long as employment avails for U.S. workers and federal income tax collection codes remain in tact, you'll never have to worry about the U.S. not paying you back if you buy some of her bonds."

New York Bank Run

Inept banking is what prompt a demand for the Federal Reserve Bank System. This monetary scheme reached self-realization in 1907 during the New York bank run. U.S. citizens lined up to retrieve their gold held by ill-managed banks. I say gold because during those years, U.S. currency was backed by gold. (See 1907 image of $10.00 gold certificate below.)

[7] www.taxtyranny.ca/articles.inc.php?command=show&ID=13420

Use of the gold certificate was from 1882 to 1933 in the United States as a form of paper currency. For instance, if you had a $10.00 bill, it would read "**Ten Dollars In Gold Coin**", which meant you could exchange your paper currency at a bank for the gold value of its worth. Each certificate gave the holder title to its corresponding amount in gold coin. America's US Treasury Department once collateralized her currency with actual gold, but not today.

Then after 1933, a new paper currency was created—the Federal Reserve Note or fiat money as shown beneath. It is this type of bill that has no real asset value, except perhaps the motto, "*In God We Trust.*"

At any rate, as the story goes surrounding the 1907 bank run, F. Augustus Heinze, a descendant of German Jewish immigrants attempted to corner the copper market by shorting the stock of a major copper company. In other words, he borrowed the stock to convive that its price would fall. After Heinze's failed scam was exposed, it generated a major bank crisses in New York City.

> *"The crisis was triggered by the failed attempt in October 1907 to corner the market on stock of the United Copper Company. When this bid failed, banks that had lent money to the cornering scheme suffered runs that later spread to affiliated banks and trusts, leading a week later to the downfall of the Knickerbocker Trust Company—New York City's third-largest trust. The collapse of the Knickerbocker spread fear throughout the city's trusts as regional banks withdrew reserves from New York City banks. Panic extended across the nation as vast numbers of people withdrew deposits from their regional banks."*[8]

Knickerbocker Trust Bank

In view of this historical event, what occurred in 1907 is similar to events that occurred during the time when Senator Barak Obama was campaigning. New York's Stock market corruption, stock shorting, housing and bank fraud, in one sense, crashed the Caucasian world's usurious-

[8] http://en.wikipedia.org/wiki/Panic_of_1907

based paper money system. Weather or not these events were contrived or not, America and Britain's best financial wizards cannot manage the criminal outfit they fortified based upon 16th century European monetary policies. So now are advocates of Talmudic finanical concepts planning to replace an outdated system with a new equitable system, *emphatically not!* Putting makeup on a pig does not change the pig, which is what the new US and global financial reform notion represents.

> WASHINGTON (Reuters) - The House of Representatives on Wednesday approved a landmark overhaul of financial regulations but the Senate put off action until mid-July, delaying a final victory for President Barack Obama.
>
> Still, the 237 to 192 vote in the House marked a win for Obama and his fellow Democrats, who have made the most sweeping rewrite of Wall Street rules since the 1930's a top priority in the wake of the 2007-2009 financial crisis.[9]

Communism In America

I once heard Minister Jabril Muhammad of Mosque 32 teach that the Honorable Elijah Muhammad said, [paraphasing] before America falls, she will be ruled for one year under Communism before finally collasping. So the question is:

[9] http://news.yahoo.com/s/nm/us_financial_regulation

if America forecloses on her promise to pay foreign investors, will Communism rule the U.S. outright. You ask, what is communism:

> *"Communism is a social structure in which classes are abolished and property is commonly controlled, as well as a political philosophy and social movement that advocates and aims to create such a society."*[10]

With certain white Moslem Sons (Shriners) now fighting from behind the eightball to prevent Communism (sale of the labor of the proletarians to the bourgeoisie) from dictating U.S. labor protections, mankind's satanic forces operating from within and without the US government are vying to eliminate what is commonly referred to the middle working class. Do you think the housing market fiasco was an accident? Who really got played. Moreover, who really owns the land beneath our feet?

Old money international investment houses as well as new money international investment houses do not care about American taxpayer lamentations about "our standard of living". International investment houses refuse to accept losing their profits vis-à-vis working class income tax

[10] http://en.wikipedia.org/wiki/Communism

collections. Their loans and profits are fixed through U.S. bonds (rentes) of every sort with a guarantee profit predetermined by the US government.

Chapter II

Mr. Christian Banker

How could it be that in 1893, one American businessman, J.P. Morgan, was not only New York City's wealthiest and most well-connected banker, he also helped rescue the U.S. Treasury Department during the bank panic in 1893?

Then again, in 1907-08 Mr. Morgan was the agent who attempted to save New York City from total collapse. Who or what was he up against? At first, he and his banking colleagues were at war against a 650-year old tradition of Europe's most experienced Talmudic Jewish money-lending networks (Joint Stock Companies), until later when Mr. Morgan "et al" came to realize "if you can't beat 'em, join 'em. Thus, usurious debt instruments became the legal commercial order the day, in America, by 1933.

Although a few elite and well-educated Americans voluntarily surrendered to Europe's medieval usurious debt finance system, on paper in 1913, she is the daughter of England. From that year onward, the power of the beast was transferred to North America between Washington DC and New York City.

The difference between Anglo American bankers and Talmudic Jewish bankers is America's banking schools of thought relied mainly on the New Testament Bible attempting to uphold early Christian lending canons. That is to say, early Christians were aware to the dangers of excess usury. To the contrary, modern day Christians are so ignorant, apathetic and superstitious they have not a clue as to how to free themselves from privatized federalized usurious debt instruments. Therefore, by their ignorance, Christian America lost complete control over what many call their sovereign nation.

As fantastic as it may seem, the federal monetary entity of the West is the beast. It was mentioned in the Christian Bible book of revelations centuries ago.

By 1913, very powerful influential Caucasian families, belonging to America's market-wise and Europe's market-wise, formed a league or treaty. They derived an agreement or covenant between certain parties to constitute by a compact, under what is now commonly known as Federal Reserve Bank, which is a quasi government of international money lenders. In total, this class of people number around 10% of the population on the planet in terms of wealth consolidation. Some reports made on

MSNBC News have said this group holds nearly 150 trillion dollars worth of assets in the U.S. alone.

> *"In terms of types of financial wealth, the top one percent of households have 38.3% of all privately held stock, 60.6% of financial securities, and 62.4% of business equity. The top 10% have 80% to 90% of stocks, bonds, trust funds, and business equity, and over 75% of non-home real estate. Since financial wealth is what counts as far as the control of income-producing assets, we can say that just 10% of the people own the United States of America."*[11]

Quasi-government central banks were established to maintain aggressive and cruel world dominance if and when necessary to order men and women into commercial nations as an artificial legal Person or consumer slave. It's nature and function is to relegate human beings as mere assets of labor and industrial tools for production of goods and services. In addition to this, each Person shall in one way or another function like an income tax "ATM Machine" for bondholders of U.S. debt. Of course, bondholders consist of the

---

[11] http://sociology.ucsc.edu/whorulesamerica/power/wealth.html

international elite financial institutions and/or moneychangers.[12]

"And Jesus went into the temple of God, and cast out all them that sold and bought in the temple, and overthrew the tables of the moneychangers, and the seats of them that sold doves, And said unto them, It is written, My house shall be called the house of prayer; but ye have made it a den of thieves."(Matthew 21:12-13)

These same satanic merchant entities are those whom overturned Jesus' mission 2,000 years ago as he attempted to bring in existence a better world for all people. Therefore, the ancient holy people described the nature of westernized culture, including its central bank apparatus' in the role of a beast.

*"And when he had taken the book, **the four beasts** and four and twenty elders **fell down** before the Lamb, having every one of them harps, and golden vials full of odours, which are the prayers of saints." (Revelation 5:8)*

*"**And the four beasts said, Amen.** And the four and twenty elders **fell down** and worshipped him that liveth for ever and ever." (Revelation 5:14)*

---

[12] Antiquity used temples to store and protect its nations wealth. The temple represented a solid building and was constantly attended by the holy persons or priest of that nation.

America's role during these end times is to maintain the usurious monetary policies of the beast by force of warfare until God's final word is accomplished.

One problem millions of white Christians, Negro preachers and/or never *the* wiser refuse to accept nothing is occurring today outside of divine scripture. America, England, Germany and Italy are foremost enforcers of excess usury and misery over the poor. However, such human beings engineering our current world economy and political order shall bow down willingly or unwillingly {Rev 5:14} "*And the four beasts said, Amen*".

I reiterate, from its entire historical scope, the ruling money elite best fit the nature of a beast in biblical speech. They devoured usury as to prey upon the weak, poor and ignorant early pagan tribes of Europe of yesteryears and commonplace people of today. Moreover, in exchange for westernized perpetual debt and inflationary finance, third world nations are forced to sell their birthright (land and resources) for food aid and a modicum of modernity.

To make matters worse, nearly 400 years of free African slave labor accounts for why Gentiles and Jews quickly grew so rich and powerful after 15th century down into the industrial age of steel and electricity.

We know what Christians taught during the Atlantic slave trade, in terms of Blacks being the descendant of Noah's son, Ham. What about the Jews, what were they taught in the Synagogue about Blacks? Minister Don Muhammad, Minister of Muhammad Mosque #11, Boston MA. Writes:

> ...the center of the rum and slave trade, all Jewish families owned Black slaves; the Touro synagogue was built by Black slaves "of some skill"; and of the 22 distilleries serving the slave trade all 22 were owned by Jewish merchants.
>
> The sad reality is that one can go on and on without much difficulty in enumerating the extensive involvement of Jews in the Black-slave trade. Actually, one is hard-pressed to name one (just one) prominent colonial American Jew who did not own slaves. He will have the same difficulty as the Anti-Defamation League had in their 1976 pamphlet entitled, American Jews: Their Story. The ADL lists 13 pioneers of the American Jewish community--10 of whom have been definitively linked to the slave trade![13]

[13] www.ety.com/HRP/slavery/blacksandjews.htm

The scandal here is Jews who voice being in bondage under a wicked Pharaoh and a satanic Nebuchadnezzar perpetuated the same inhumane vile crime against Black Africa.

Although Western capitalism offers the best modern conveniences known to mankind, this world is built upon slavery, suffering, usury-debt and every sort of financial crime against humanity that contest the law of Islam. Why did the people of the Synagogue capitulate with Satan is the question?

Oldest European Banks On Earth

Enumerated below are Europe's oldest banks. A cursory review of each bank's history evinces how wickedly wise merchants and rulers decided to operate financially like criminals.

- ***Banca Monte dei Paschi di Siena Siena, Italy.*** *Established in 1472 to grant loans to "poor or miserable or needy persons," Monte di Pieta, or Monte Pio as it was then known, translates as mountain of piety.*

- ***Berenberg Bank Hamburg, Germany.*** *Germany's oldest private bank was founded in 1590 by Hans and Paul Berenberg, cloth traders from Antwerp who fled religious persecution in Holland to settle in Hamburg.*

- ***Bank of Sweden Stockholm, Sweden.*** *Sveriges Riksbank is the world's oldest central bank, responsible for conducting monetary policy and issuing Sweden's official banknotes. The first real banknotes were issued by Stockholm Banco in 1661 by founder Johan Palmstruch who came up with the idea of facilitating the management of money by issuing "credit notes," interest-free IOUs in specific amounts that were meant to correspond to money deposited in the bank.* ***The banknotes were a great success, though the bank eventually failed after Palmstruch issued too many notes in the form of unsecured loans.***

As you can see, this world's bank cartels have had many blueprints prepared before them. My question is: were there enough examples to enable the cartels to prevent financial collapses and/or to make heaven on earth with God's wealth? By today's finanical debacle, the ungrateful sinners bent toward collapse. The Quran warns: "*So, the one who receives an admonition from his Sustainer and thereby desists (from usury) riba, may keep his past gains; his affairs are with Allah. But he that returns to (riba) usury shall be among the people of the Fire forever.* "*Allah deprives the gains of all blessings through riba (usury), whereas He blesses charitable deeds with manifold increase. And Allah bears no love for the ungrateful sinner.*"*(Quran, 2: 276)*

Further, you will read more about Europe's oldest banks:

- ***C. Hoare and Co. London, England.*** *Established in 1672 by Sir Richard Hoare, the bank began as a goldsmith under the sign of the golden bottle in Cheapside. Goldsmiths had secure premises and had always been the storehouses for cash and valuables. With the recent repeal of usury laws, which banned the lending of money for interest, Richard Hoare was able to begin lending money to customers for interest. The bank remains a family-owned and -managed bank, the sole survivor of the private deposit banks, which were established in the 17th and 18th centuries.*

- ***Halifax Bank of Scotland*** *Edinburgh, Scotland. The Bank of Scotland was established in 1695 by an Act of the Scottish Parliament, the first bank to be established in Scotland, and one of the first in the UK. In 1696, Bank of Scotland became the first bank in Europe to successfully issue paper currency. These first notes were issued in denominations of £5, £10, £50 and £100 - the first £1 note did not appear until 1704. The Bank's right to issue notes has been maintained to the present day.*

- ***The Bank of New York Mellon New York.*** *The bank began with a small advertisement in The New York Packet announcing plans to start New York's first bank. Eight years later, it was the first company to be traded publicly when the New York Stock Exchange opened in 1792. The bank's* *constitution was written by Alexander Hamilton, who envisioned an institution that would support the goals of the government, address the needs of the local merchants and residents and spur the growth and development of the community at large. For the first 15 years of its existence, the bank financed virtually all of New York City's commercial activity, and most importers of cargo entering the Port of New York turned to the Bank for financing. The bank helped fund the Morris and Erie Canals and financed the steamboat companies that sailed those waterways. As the industrial age took hold, the bank invested in nearly every railroad and utility, as well as in the construction of the New York City subway system. In 2007, the bank merged with the Mellon Company, which as T. Mellon and Sons of Pittsburgh had provided backing for such companies as US Steel, Alcoa and Westinghouse in the early days of their founding.*[14]

The founding fathers of America and her financial magnets never stood a chance to combat against Europe's criminal bank cartel invasion. It was apparent from the days of the 13 colonies that no American businessman or politicain understood how to defend nor create a stable bank system for their nation.

For example, Robert Morris, the reknowned slave holder, politician and first Superintendent of Finance of the United

[14] http://blog.nationalpayday.com/banks/oldest-banks-world/

States, is partly responsible for the creation of the first financial institution chartered by the United States, the Bank of North America, in 1782. He failed miserably. The bank was funded in part by a significant loan Morris had obtained from France in 1781. The initial role of the bank was to finance the war against Britain.[15]

However, due to Morris' global short-sitedness greed, arogance and sense of entitlement, he got involved in too many unsuccessful land speculations; at the wrong time in history, and ended up in prison for owing debt. In fact, it was this gentlemans bludder that bankrupcy came into practice.

"The subsequent Napoleonic Wars ruined the market for American Lands and Morris's highly leveraged company collapsed. The financial markets of England, the United States, and the Caribbean were also suffering from the deflation associated with the Panic of 1797. Thus Morris was land-poor (he owned much land but didn't have enough hard money to pay off his creditors).

"Although he attempted to avoid his creditors by remaining at "The Hills", his country estate on the Schuylkill River in Philadelphia, his creditors

[15] http://en.wikipedia.org/wiki/Robert_Morris_(financier)

literally pursued him to his gate. After he was sued by a former partner, a fraud who at that time was serving time in debtor's prison himself, he was arrested and imprisoned for debt in Prune Street prison in Philadelphia from February 1798 to August 1801...

"Morris's economic failure reduced the fortunes of many other prominent Federalists who had invested in his ventures (e.g., Henry Lee). Morris's political adversaries used his bankruptcy to gain political power in Pennsylvania...

"Congress passed the Bankruptcy Laws, in part, to get Morris out of prison."[16]

To what do we owe this great American, Robert Morris for his finanical blunderings? His picture was added to the U.S. $1000.00 Bill from 1862 to 1863.

---

[16] http://en.wikipedia.org/wiki/Robert_Morris_(financier)

Chapter III

U.S. Bankers Failed

During the 18th century, the United States created two major banks. The Bank of the U.S. was set up to handle the monetary affairs of the federal government, than came *The Second Bank of the United States*. These two chartered for 20 years before going bankrupt in 1841. The first and second bank of North America were only an experiment.

"The First Bank of United States was in no sense a national bank but rather a privately held banking corporation. The bank had a unique relationship with the federal government that gave it access to substantial profits. Its role as the depository of the federal government's revenues made it a political target of banks chartered by the individual states who objected/envied the First Bank of United States's relationship with the central government. Partisan politics came heavily into play in the debate over the renewal of the charter.

"The classic statement by Arthur Schlesinger was that the partisan politics saw inter-party conflict as a clash between wealthy Whigs and working class Democrats (Grynaviski). President Andrew

Jackson strongly opposed the renewal of its charter, and built his platform for the election of 1832 around doing away with the Second Bank of the United States.[17]

Good suspicion said to most hard working people that bank credit was hard to attain because *wealthy Whigs* were only lending to insiders and family members whom they trusted to invest. Yet these banks held deposits of hard working people too.

From the very beginning, Banks of the U.S. failed the test. One banking problem during the 1800's was 50 different currencies were in circulation. It was obvious to market-wise observers in Europe that America's monetary ideals were like amature time in Dixie. America's monetary policy was in chaos. Depending upon what state one resided, the currency might have been English, Spanish, French, or Portuguese coinage. And in various cities, where mom and pop shops and small enterprises accepted such coins as a median of exchange, coin values were not only unknown but unknowable as one historian put it.

This confusion and monetary experimentation is exactly what

---

[17] http://en.wikipedia.org/wiki/Second_bank_of_the_united_states

international bank cartel's needed to know to gain an advantage. So the argument for a central bank apparatus whereby nations grow and prosper was in demand. Therefore, the idea of employing a universally accepted standard coinage gained moral ground in the U.S.

When the moment arrived for Europe's central bank apparatus to put all local and state U.S. banks throughtout the land under one federal regulatory supervision board, no oppostion stymied their agenda. People only wanted an acceptable medium to exchange goods and services.

Civil War

Since the future pointed to America, and U.S. secret societal government leaders of the Masonic order began to realize their destiny; on an international scale, physical slavery had to also end. In view of the future, in 1787, the 3/5ths compromise was presented in the constitution in Article 1, Section 2, Paragraph 3 of the United States Constitution. It states: ***"Representatives and direct Taxes shall be apportioned among the several States which may be included within this Union, according to their respective Numbers, which shall be determined by adding to the whole Number of free Persons, including those bound to Service for a Term of Years, and***

excluding Indians not taxed, three fifths of all other Persons." The legal jargon above was not only written to prevent America's southern slave states from paying more taxes than they had preferred, but also to inform them taxes must be paid for the number of human bodies on the land. There the South immediately objected to this formula since it would include slaves, who were viewed primarily as property, in calculating the amount of taxes to be paid. What ensued was war!

> "***Following the Civil War and the abolition of slavery*** *by the Thirteenth Amendment to the United States Constitution (1865),* ***the three-fifths clause was rendered moot.*** *Section 2 of the Fourteenth Amendment to the United States Constitution (1868) later superseded Article 1, Section 2, Clause 3. It specifically states that "Representatives shall be apportioned ...counting the whole number of persons in each State, excluding Indians not taxed..."*[18]

Although the lost people of God—Black America were held in slavery 400 years and set back in terms of their financial gains, our ancient forefathers did not intend

[18] http://en.wikipedia.org/wiki/Three-fifths_compromise

for Western Europe's new world order to totally destroy the African slave population into oblivion. That is why America could not escape the ultimate monetary policies dictated to her by the international Bankers. Her opportunity to right the wrong for slavery came and left in 1776, when America gained independence from the British Empire. Instead of setting the slaves free, America waited until 1964 to pass a civil rights bill that is now almost worthless in today's new international order.

At any rate, *The Federal Reserve Act* of 1913 ushered in our present day privatized Federal Reserve central money lending entity to charge or tax or levy and regulate all U.S. taxpayers. This entity (Federal Reserve) was designed to inveigle every living man, women and child under a privatized-monetary jurisdiction governed by Talmudic writings controlled by self-righteous hypocrites and disbelievers in All Mighty Allah (God). We could also say, Bank wars, in our modern times, is like a war between God and Satan—Jesus and the moneychangers. The question is: whose side do you stand?

Today, there are 12 twelve regional Federal Reserve Banks that are supervised by a Federal Reserve Board. This particular monetary system has been used to prolong the Adamic civilization (or Caucasian rule) over the aboriginal nations of the earth beyond its 6,000-year rule.

Map (A) locates the 12 Federal Reserve Headquarters throughout America called districts. This structure was put in place to maintain the rule of law over the masses and take a *doomsday* account to what is owed to the Central Bank.

Map (A)

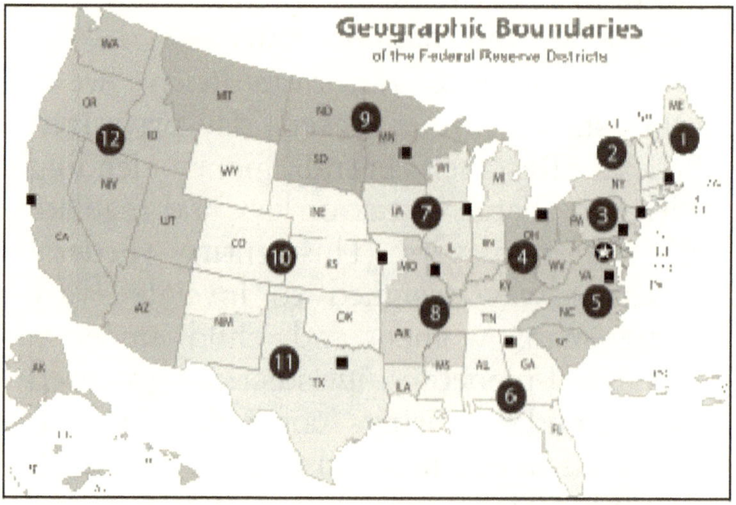

There is no mystery God in the sky and the people have surely given the beast its due. This is why the Bible books of Acts 5:3-4 reads: "[3]*Ananias, how is it that Satan has so filled your heart that you have lied to the Holy Spirit and have kept for yourself some of the money you received for the land?* [4]*Didn't it belong to you before it [seigniorage] was sold? And after it was sold,*

wasn't the money [seigniorage] at your disposal? What made you think of doing such a thing? You have not lied to men but to God."

Human Surety Insurance

During the turn of century, all U.S. persons (black, white and all in between) were re-classified as a "surety", which made central bankers comfortable buying U.S. bonds (rentes). A surety is a person (or company) who agrees to be responsible for the debt or obligation of another i.e. the spend-happy US Federal Government. Furthermore, a surety is also a security against loss (Insurance).

Market-wise central bankers craved to maximize rentes from every able-bodied man and women on earth. To make their plan more palatable in the US market, money market certain controls were executed under the "In God We Trust" motto. The god Bankers trust is taxpayers working within the domain of the "royal crown".

Fraught, U.S. working class people had to be sold out by elected political leaders to make modern day money-changers enjoy a successful outcome with usurious profits {Mathew 23:14} "...*Ye devour widows' houses. Devour their property under holy pretenses.*" What is happening in the United States is nothing new.

Hence, under Central Bank *financial* rules of law, every living man is considered a fictional or legal Person existing in westernized commercial nations. Under the rules of finance, the working class must remain in debt for life to enjoy modernity as opposed to third world conditions.

As far as secret society members are concerned, every man, women, child and unborn have a privilege to access conveniences provided via commercial USA. And for these conveniences, three hundred million plus Americans owes $42,000 each as our bill on the US national debt. Some arrogant secret society types will say, 'If you don't like it, leave to country! Their thinking is derived from the Bible book of Numbers 18:14-15, wherein it says, "[14]*Every devoted thing in Israel shall be yours.* [15]*Everything that first opens the womb of all flesh, which they bring to the Lord, whether man or beast shall be yours: nevertheless the firstborn of man shall surely redeem, and the firstborn of unclean animals you shall redeem....*"

For the impatient people of the Western hemisphere, money became a GOD in which WE TRUST! This meant a drunken subjection to the woes of debt finance. It meant fair-seemingly exponential commercial and industrial progress and fine cars.

By engineering politicians and U.S. citizens to serve paper money above God, "a criminal people" gained control over the land and sea promising a progress in North America like no other secular civilization before it in the annuals of time.

Curse and Blessing of Fiat Money

For the longest time, the U.S. dollar has been declining since 1774 as shown in the following examples:

$36.32 in the year 1774 has the same "purchase power" as **$1000** in the year 2008.

Conversely, if you took '08 money value back to year 1774, *$27,532* dollars would be equivalent to only *$1000.00 in value.*

$137.57 in the year 1960 has the same "purchase power" as **$1000** in the year 2008.

Conversely, if you took '08 money value back to year 1960, *$7,268.84* dollars would be would be equivalent to only *$1000.00 in value.*

$250.07 in the year 1975 has the same "purchase power" as **$1000** in the 2008.

Conversely, if you took "08 money value back to year 1975, *$3,998.94* dollars would be would be equivalent to only *$1000.00* in value.

Clearly, you can see how America's "purchase power" has fallen year after year after year. These figures were calculated by measuringworth.com by analyzing *the who, what, when, where, how and why* economic indicators as to peoples spending habits. Human basic needs have not changed, only the value of our purchase power.

I reiterate, the Federal Reserve System was a curse and a blessing for Europe's new world built in North America rooted in murder, slavery and debt finance. Yet, this type of world order was permitted to fulfill a divine plan prewritten in both Bible and Quran to show both man and mankind what each is made of.

The key reason why U.S. paper money is losing value lie between its financial relationship with the Federal Reserve monetary controllers, compromised DC insiders and the Supreme U.S. court.

Chapter IV
God Is Not Anti-Loan

Today although the U.S. Treasury Department informs the U.S. Mint to print paper money and coins, every paper dollar has attached to it a usurious interest rate that "we the people" must pay to the Federal Reserves network of elite shareholders—hidden owners.

D.C. Federal Reserve Temple

Ironically the Federal Reserve is the only authority that may give the Treasury Department an order to print money. All federal income taxes are then collected by the Internal Revenue Service (IRS), whom informs tax payers to make his or her check out to the U.S. Treasury Department. If one is late paying taxes to the private owners of the IRS, a late interest fee will be charged to your tax bill, interest upon interest until all taxes are paid in full. Why? Because each U.S. Person was made a surety under the Federal Reserve Act of 1913.

White Americans hated paying taxes as early as 1862.

"1862 - President Lincoln signed into law a revenue-raising measure to help pay for Civil War expenses. The

measure created a Commissioner of Internal Revenue and the nation's first income tax. It levied a 3 percent tax on incomes between $600 and $10,000 and a 5 percent tax on incomes of more than $10,000."

"1913 *- As the threat of war loomed, Wyoming became the 36th and last state needed to ratify the 16th Amendment. The amendment stated, "Congress shall have the power to lay and collect taxes on incomes, from whatever source derived, without apportionment among the several states, and without regard to any census or enumeration." Later, Congress adopted a 1 percent tax on net personal income of more than $3,000 with a surtax of 6 percent on incomes of more than $500,000. It also repealed the 1909 corporate income tax. The first Form 1040 was introduced."*[19]

We are many years away when 3% taxation was charged for government expenditures.

From year 2000 to 2010, the large sums of money borrowed by states, cities, manufacturers, corporations, small businesses, students, homeowners and the U.S. government from the Federal Reserve System apparatus have actually trapped U.S. taxpayers into perpetual debt because the Federal Reserve usurious interest rates are mathematically designed to compound interest on the principle amount of each loan issued to the U.S. government.

---

[19] http://www.cookco.us/historical_highlights_of_the_irs.htm

Allah (God) is not against loans. God is against compounding interest rates on loans, which is usurious, a devouring usury!

"Compound interest arises when interest is added to the principal, so that from that moment on, the interest that has been added also itself earns interest. This addition of interest to the principal is called compounding (i.e. the interest is compounded).

"A loan, for example, may have its interest compounded every month: in this case, a loan with $100 initial principal and 1% interest per month would have a balance of $101 at the end of the first month, $102.01 at the end of the second month, and so on." Put another way, the borrower is charged interest on previous interest.[20]

Largely, the nature of the Federal Reserve System's monetary policy is Satanic. It is anti-Christ.

The monetary policy of the Federal Reserve System might have succeeded, except for their greed and exploitative lending practices went beyond the boundaries of usury. Imagine charging interest on interest on interest on previous interest. This is criminal in the mind of Allah (God).

On the other side of the coin, however, today if you are a Wall Street insider or fortunate investor who follows the money, you may earn profits galore.

---

[20] http://en.wikipedia.org/wiki/Compound_interest

Even so, excess usury (the borrower is charged interest on previous interest) has devoured the true wealth and purchase power of the people. Talmudic monetary power and control or Master/slave rule over the ignorant is on the margin of economic failure.

Make no mistake about it, in 1913 U.S. Congressional powers surrendered it's monetary authority into the hands of an international bank cartel of elite Caucasians permitting them to print and to loan money to America without any solid asset other than an agreement U.S. working class income taxpayers will be the surety.

Currently, nearly 35% of every U.S. citizens purchase power is appropriated by Congress to guarentee tax collections to pay upon an unending national debt. No matter how much is wasteful spending and unneccessary war engagements, every working Person must pay his or her share of national taxes to meet an impossible U.S. debt obligation.

"A number of things are coming to a head among Russia, China, Brazil, and the Gulf states, including their own growth, the FED's policies, the troubled US banking system and economy, the extended US military positions, and the impossible debt obligations of the US government

for social programs. Other countries as well have greater incentives to lower their acceptance of the dollar and increase their acceptance of gold and/or other currencies that have higher gold backing. This fourth factor is incipient [just beginning] but growing."[21]

Debt Financing

Debt financing is financing a company or government by selling the bonds, notes or mortgages held by the business. Debt financing is borrowing money to keep your business doors open.

Long term debt financing is typically associated with larger assets such as buildings, equipment, land, and large machinery. A city or state cannot function without businesses, corporations, end-users, public transportation, a labor force, etc. All of these elements represent tax revenues.

Each city or state's endurance depends upon every business and Legal Fiction Person under its jurisdiction to pay some form of taxes. If businesses and homeowners suffer debt, cities and states also suffer because they depend upon tax collections of some kind from the people also.

[21] http://www.marketoracle.co.uk/Article14168.html

Primarily every viable business entity within a city or a state must initially pay interest on everything it needs to generate energy. For what its worth, everything purchased is manufactured with debt finance and debt finance always carries an interest rate. Then those interest rates are absorbed and always past onto the consumer.

In modern commercialized nations, cities and states are in business and must borrow money to remain open for business. Today due to hard times, many states and cities cannot pay down their loans, floating bonds or municipal bonds.

To make matters turn for the worse, job loss has meant lack of tax collections, which is why cutting social programs and salaries, education, raising property and sales taxes is happening and will continue to increase.

Budget cuts are designed to reduce what might have been converted into pay raises and more employment stimulus to help pay down interest rates on previous loans (more commonly called floating bonds and municipal bonds) for cities and states. Again, these type of bonds are sold by cities and states to governments and international investment houses to maintain stability. The lack of jobs means the lack of tax collection, which means little hope of receiving new loans at lower interest rates.

Is America Headed Into Revolution?

Is White America headed into revolution? I have provided only a small example of some U.S. cities debt levels.

Detroit 2009

$300 million deficit, mostly because of a decrease in property and income taxes, plus the cost to run city services and pay city workers. ***Michigan State*** 23.2 billion of *debt*

Chicago 2009

Debt $420 Million

Illionos State

$25 billion of debt

Los Angeles 2009

98.1 million in the red.

California State

net tax-supported debt

$61 billion

New York 2009

Debt is $64.9 billion

New York State

$140 billion in debt

As you can see, what a fine mess so-called elite white folks have built upon illusions of grandeur via debt finance.

Both America and Europe face grim budget deficits because what is, partially, financed through taxation [has been] the gigantic bureaucracy to administer a welfare state of existance. These states actual provision of "security" is made, in its entirety, through borrowing, facilitated through the operations of Central Banks and national Treasuries or Ministries of Finance.

Subsequently, western governments, cities and states have spent more money than their economy's value has in productivity.

Many Hip Hop fans once touted the phase "Cream" meaning "*Cash Rules Every Thing Around Me.*" Well the following statistics demonstrate the CREAM by which the market-wise has measured their economic growth and strength since 1914 to 2010.

- U.S. official gold reserves, totaling 261.5 million troy ounces, have a book value as of 30 November 2009 of approximately $11 billion, vs. a commodity value as of 17 December 2009 of approximately $288.5 billion.

- Foreign exchange reserves $134 million as of October 2009.

- The Strategic Petroleum Reserve had a value of approximately $69 billion as of December 2009, at a Market Price of $104/barrel with a $15/barrel discount for sour crude.

- The national debt equates to $30,400 per person U.S. population, or $60,100 per head of the U.S. working population, as of February 2008.

- In 2008, $242 billion was spent on interest payments servicing the debt, out of a total tax revenue of $2.5 trillion, or 9.6%. Including non-cash interest accrued primarily for Social Security, interest was $454 billion or 18% of tax revenue.

- Total U.S. household debt, including mortgage loan and consumer debt, was $11.4 trillion in 2005. By comparison, total U.S. household assets, including real estate, equipment, and financial instruments such as mutual funds, was $62.5 trillion in 2005.

- Total U.S Consumer Credit Card revolving credit debt was $931.0 billion in April 2009.

- Total third world debt was estimated to be $1.3 trillion in 1990.

- The U.S. balance of trade deficit in goods and services was $725.8 billion in 2005.

- The global market capitalization for all stock markets that are members of the World Federation of Exchanges was $32.5 trillion by the end of 2008.[22] [Note: $100 trillion if truth be told]

Historically speaking, debt was responsible for the creation of medeival indentured servants. Nowadays it's the Federal Reserve System repeating history. Although some exclaim, "*at least we the people*" get an annual income tax check for our labor, those days may be numbered. Let us hope not because we all need money.

To continue living the American life style of abundance and to enjoy all its conforts compared to third world nations, however, federal income taxes must be

[22] http://en.wikipedia.org/wiki/United_States_public_debt

increased to meet what is owed to central banks and other U.S. bondholders. Yet the debt can never be repaid because the *Banksters* interest rate formula is ever compounding.

"Whatever usury you offer to grow in people's wealth will not grow with God ..."(Quran 30:39).

Unfortunately, U.S. income tax dollars can never pay off her interest fees racked up by the U.S. governments evil spending habits that in turn require the federal central bank to inforce more borrowing inordinately. In vain, since 1914, a world of illusions has been hoisted before the nations like all is well. Finally, this illusion is exposed and fading away.

"[20] ***Know that this worldly life is no more than play and games, and boasting among you, and hoarding of money and children.*** *It is like abundant rain that produces plants and pleases the disbelievers. But then, the plants turn into useless hay, and are blown away by the wind. In the Hereafter, there is either severe retribution, or forgiveness from GOD and approval.* ***This worldly life is no more than a temporary illusion.*** [21]*Therefore, you shall race towards forgiveness from your Lord, and a Paradise whose width encompasses the heaven and the earth. It awaits those who believed in GOD and His messengers. Such is GOD's grace that He bestows upon whomever He wills. GOD is Possessor of Infinite Grace.* [22]*Anything that happens on earth, or to you, has already been recorded, even before the creation. This is easy for GOD to do." (Quran 57:20-22)*

Chapter V

What Is Usury

Civilizations of antiquity used temples to store and protect its nations wealth. The temple represented a solid building and was constantly attended by the holy persons or priest of that nation. Their presence alone deterred thieves and robbers. In Babylon at the time of Hammurabi, in the 18th century BC, temples occupied a most important position too.

According to Claude Hermann Walter Johns study of the BABYLONIAN LAW--The Code of Hammurabi from the Eleventh Edition of the Encyclopedia Britannica, 1910-1911 he writes: "Hammurabi was the ruler who chiefly established the greatness of Babylon, the world's first metropolis. Many relics of Hammurabi's reign ([1795-1750 BC]) have been preserved, and today we can study this remarkable King.... as a wise lawgiver in his celebrated code. It received from its estates, from tithes and other fixed dues, as well as from the sacrifices (a customary share) and other offerings of the faithful, vast amounts of all sorts of naturalia; besides money and permanent gifts. The larger temples had many officials and servants. Originally, perhaps, each town clustered round one temple, and each head of a family had a right to minister there and share its receipts... In spite of all these demands, however, the temples became great granaries and storehouses; as they also were the city archives.

"The temple held its responsibilities. If a citizen was captured by the enemy and could not ransom himself the temple of his city must do so. To the temple came the poor farmer to borrow seed corn or supplies for harvesters, and advances, which, he repaid without interest. The king's power over the temple was not proprietary but administrative".

Clearly, the Temple represented the Central Bank of the ancient Babylonian world. On the contrary, the order of the monetary policy employed today is unlike any nation before it, including that of the Babylonian ruler, Hammurabi. For the Temple or Central Bank apparatus of our times is controlled by the Synagogue of Satan.

In modern western financed cities, millions are surrounded by concrete, electricity and steel. People are steadfast to be proud of deceitfulness and lying. Millions decrease from feeling God's urge from within, but rather increase to feel and need an urge for money by any means necessary!

So not only are the monetary policies unnatural, but men and women have become different toward one another in unnatural ways just to get their hands on "*In God We Trust.*"

Most people spend five to six days per week geared up to earn enough wages to pay bills on a thirty-day cycle. Perhaps to prevent some material goods like a home or car from being reprocessed or to prevent lights, water or power from being turned off. For these reasons, and then some, "In God We Trust" keeps far too many in stress, strain and worry until death due us part.

In retrospect, that which the Federal Reserve System wrought in 1913-1933 appeared like an angel to a distressed and young economy. Nevertheless, it really embodied death to the economy, yet life too although it is an illusion rooted in counterfeit.

Overall, what America's budding governmental administrators thought was economic reproduction; namely, for white folks has now become economic destruction. Western capitalism is boom and bust usury economics and financial mathematical tricks worked within the Temple—modern day central banking institutions. Did they know better? Of course!

"What do Hammurabi, Plato, Charlemagne, Dante and Queens Mary and Elizabeth have in common? They all condemned, outlawed or regulated the charging of interest on loans. In fact, until the early 1900s interest rates in the United States were kept at or near 10%. And until 1979, loan laws provided some interest rate cap in every state. Then everything changed. Governments and banks put profits before people. And now the lending industry is spiraling out of control.

"What is Usury?

1. *The practice of lending money and charging the borrower interest, especially at an exorbitant or illegally high rate.*
2. *An excessive or illegally high rate of interest charged on borrowed money.*
3. *Archaic. Interest charged or paid on a loan".*

"The Prophet Ezekiel includes usury in a list of "abominable things," along with rape, murder, robbery and idolatry. Ezekiel 18:19-13.

Jews are forbidden to lend at interest to one another. Exodus 22:25; Deuteronomy 23:19-20, Leviticus 25:35-37.

"**1750 B.C.** *The Code of Hammurabi regulates the interest that can be charged on a loan. Historical records indicate that many loans were made below the legal limit.*

"**800-600 B.C.** *Both Plato and Aristotle believed usury was immoral and unjust. The Greeks at first regulate interest, and then deregulate it. After deregulation, there was so much unregulated debt that Athenians were sold into slavery and threatened revolt.*

"**443 B.C.** *The Romans adopt the "Twelve Tables" and cap interest at 8 1/3%.*

"**88 B.C.** *The Roman usury rate is raised to 12%.*

"**533 A.D.** *The Roman "Code of Justinian" sets a graduated maximum interest rate that did not go over 8 1/3 % for loans to ordinary citizens. This law lasts until 1543 A.D.*

"**800 A.D.** *Charlemagne outlaws interest throughout his empire.*

"**11th century** *In England, the taking of any interest at all is punishable by taking the usurer's land and chattels.*

"**Medieval Canon Law** *Usury is punishable by ex-communication.*

"**Medieval Roman Law** *Usurer's are fined 4X the amount taken, while robbery is penalized at twice the amount taken.*

"**1306-1321** *Dante pens "The Inferno," in which he places usurers at the lowest ledge in the seventh circle of hell – lower than murderers.*

"**1553-1558** *During the reign of Queen Mary, English Parliament again disallows the collection of interest.*

"**1570** *During the Reign of Queen Elizabeth, interest rates in England are limited to under 10%. This law lasts until 1854.*

"**1713** *Adoption in England of the "Statue of Anne," an Act to reduce interest rates*

"**Early 18th Century** *American colonies adopt usury laws, setting the interest cap at 8%.*

"**After 1776** *All of the States in the Union adopt a general usury. Most states set the interest limit at 6%.*

"**Early 1900s** *A move to deregulation causes 11 states to eliminate their usury laws. Nine more states raise the usury cap to 10% or 12%. Banks are not making personal loans. "Salary Lenders" fill the need by "purchasing" a worker's future wages in exchange for a high fee – equal to a lending rate of 10% - 33%.*

"**1916** *A Uniform Small Loan Law allows specially-licensed lenders to charge higher interest rates—up to 36%—in return for adhering to strict standards of lending.*

"**1945-1979** *All states adopt special loan laws that cap interest at higher than the general usury rate—at 36%—but cap it nevertheless.*

"**1978** *The US Supreme Court decides that national banks may export the state interest rate law of their home state into any state where they do business. In response, South Dakota eliminates its interest rate caps. Several credit card issuing banks move to South Dakota and operate nationally with no interest rate cap.*

"**2001-2007** *Predatory and mainly subprime lenders made home loans to people who cannot afford them, boosting their own profits in the short term. Many of these loans are packaged and sold to Wall Street.*

"**2008** *Unpaid mortgages cause mortgage-backed securities on Wall Street to continue to "go bad," triggering widespread economic downturn in both the United States and around the world. Some commercial and investment banks go bankrupt, and some are the object of government "bailouts."*[23]

Mark Of The Beast Usury Year 1672

With all of the previous history demonstrating varying degrees of laws limiting usury, who or what diabolical enterprise deregulated honest money policies, and continue to forge unjust interest rates upon the global economy.

The first European banker permitted to experiment with usury practices, after the age of enlightenment for Europeans, was Sir Richard Hoare. In 1672 Richard

[23] http://www.affil.org/consumer_rsc/usury.php

established his own bank. Prior to this effort, he sent his early life working as an apprentice for the Goldsmith's Company. This London based company was a part of the trade associations known as the Worshipful Company of the relevant trade or profession.

The Worshipful Company were responsible for the regulation of London, England's trades, controlling, for instance, wages and labour conditions and well as evaluating gold and eventually issuing paper money.

Livery Symbol

"***The Company was the medieval guild for goldsmiths, as well as silversmiths and jewellers. Only 'masters' of the company could trade in these fields in the city. The Company was originally responsible for hallmarking platinum, gold and silver.*** *(The word hallmarking arises from the fact that precious metals were officially inspected and marked in Goldsmiths' Hall, the Company's official home.) Today, the Company is one of the few Livery Companies that continues to carry out its ancient functions.* ***The Company operates the London Assay Office, where objects made of precious metals are tested for purity, and then marked with an official symbol if they pass the necessary tests.*** *At a Trial of the Pyx,* *they are responsible for checking the validity of British coinage.*"[24]

Notice the Livery Company symbol is a beast of some sort. This symbol you will find on the door of the London Assay Office of Goldsmiths, at Gutter Lane London EC2V 8AQ, United Kingdom.

During the 16th century, the Goldsmiths of London, England began the practice of holding gold of depositors and issuing receipts for gold. The receipts started to be used as paper money because people accepted them as a means of payment since they could be traded for the gold held by the Goldsmiths. Under these terms, Goldsmiths started making loans with the receipts, and in the 17th century, after realizing that only a small number of people traded their receipts for gold at any one time, started making more loans than what they had in gold. Hence, we have the beginning of fractional reserve banking i.e., lending more money than what was actually held in gold. So by deceit, Goldsmiths discovered they could create more money in which the people believed and trusted they had in Gold.

Along these lines, the craft of what is called fractional reserve banking manifested.

---

[24] http://en.wikipedia.org/wiki/Goldsmiths%27_Company

This sort of swindling or counterfeiting is dignified by the term "*fractional-reserve banking*," which means that bank deposits are backed by only a small amount of deposits. In the short run, banks (Goldsmiths) made loans to increase profits rooted in fraud. For if any failed to return the peoples gold upon return of receipts, all hell would have broken loose.

Central banks of today are mere outgrowths of what 17th century Goldsmiths had contrived to earn profits exploiting the hard work and savings of others. European goldsmiths of the Worshipful Company grossly preyed upon the unsuspecting by making illegal loans with receipts, more loans than they had value in gold hordes. Therefore, it was out that trick when a paper-deity was issued throughout Europe first and then into North America during the 1930's. America and the entire world of commercial nations are presently subdued or pegged to the paper deity labeled with the motto, "In God We Trust."

Modern central bank monetary policy; at least in the U.S., dictates the purchase power of any person who wants to buy or sell goods and services in the market place. Employment means all must register with the government at the social security office. Thereafter a number is issued enabling its carrier to enter into the market place to buy or sell goods as long as "we" spend Federal Reserve Notes.

> *"And he causeth all, both small and great, rich and poor, free and bond, to receive a mark in their right hand, or in their foreheads: and that no man might buy or sell, save he that had the mark, or the name of the beast, or the number of his name." Rev 13: 16-17*

I know some religious people use the "**Render unto Caesar...**" argument... *"Render unto Caesar the things which are Caesar's, and unto God the things that are God's"*. The issue is not whether one should pay taxes or not pay taxes or spend Federal Reserve Notes (FRN) or not spend the ill gotten note. The issue is how in the hell did the U.S. and the entire modern Christian world become subjected under a usurious beastlike monetary system controlled by the Synagogue of Satan?

With the old testament in one hand and new testment the other hand, what went wrong Mr. Christian? Simply put, God's promises of money, good homes and luxury came to slow or with much toiling. Therefore, Satanic market-wise men offered the world of mankind a tax costly yet expedious path to fulfill what we yearn that is comfort, good homes and luxury; song, dance, women, diamonds, jewells, fine clothes, sport and play. In the white mans understanding of capitalism, all must go into debt before receiving "good credit", provided all bills are paid on time.

"And Satan said when the matter was complete: "God had promised you the promise of truth, and I promised you and broke my promise. And I had no power over you except that I invited you and you responded to me. So do not blame me, but blame yourselves; I cannot help you nor can you help me. I reject that you have set me as a partner before this; the wicked will have a painful retribution." (Holy Quran 14:22)

None of the promises made by this world's monetary policy makers has prevented America's economic decline. On the next page, I have provided a U.S. debt chart, which demonstrates the hell America suffers from the ill affects of compounding interest fees owed to the Synagogue of Satan. (See chart I)

Chart I

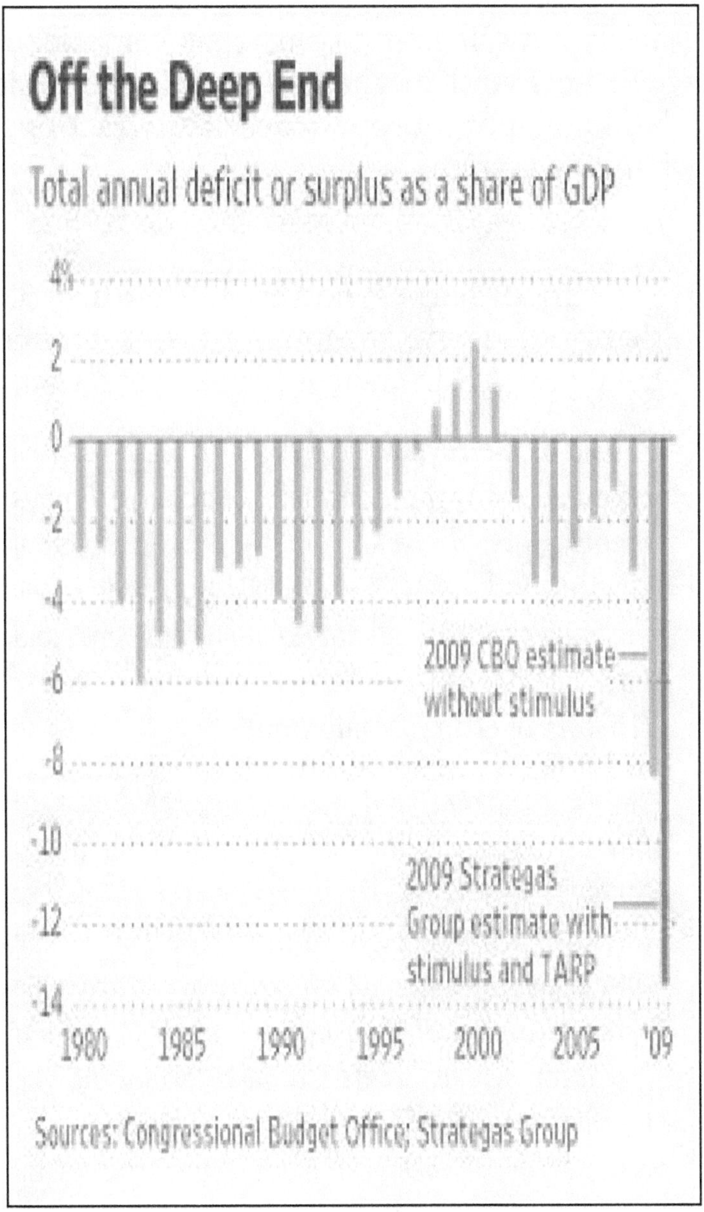
Off the Deep End
Total annual deficit or surplus as a share of GDP
4%
2
0
-2
-4
-6
-8
-10
-12
-14
1980
1985
1990
1995
2000
2005
'09
2009 CBO estimate without stimulus
2009 Strategas Group estimate with stimulus and TARP
Sources: Congressional Budget Office; Strategas Group

On chart I, everything below ground zero is debt accumulation from 1980 to 2009.

Balance is what the U.S. economy needs now. It is my belief that her balance will be found in the principles of Islamic banking, not Europe's deceitful fractional banking system.

History of Usury

In all fairnes; however, regarding the history of usury, we must go back around 2,000 years to an ancient black civilization.

> *"Some of the earliest references to usury can be observed in the ancient Indian religious manuscripts, derived from the Vedic texts of Ancient India (2,000-1,400 BC) in which the kusidin - the usurer, is stated numerous times and inferred to as any lender charging interest (History of Usury Prohibition).*

> *"More recurrent and meticulous references to interest payments can be read in the later Sutra texts (700-100 BC), alongside the Buddhist Jatakas (600-400 BC). In this latter period, the first echoes of contempt for usury are heard. One example is that of Vasishtha, a renowned Hindu legislator whom created a law forbidding the higher castes of Brahmanas (priests) and Kshatriyas (warriors) from being usurers or lenders charging interest. Also, in the Jatakas,*

usury is referred to in a derogatory tone: "hypocritical ascetics are accused of practising it" (History of Usury Prohibition).

"In the second century AD however, the term usury began to undergo a process of amelioration having become a more relative term that carries undertones which are much less harsh. In the Laws of Manu it reads:

"Stipulated interest beyond the legal rate being against (the law), cannot be recovered: they call that a usurious way (of lending)" (Jain, 1929: 3-10).[25]

Had it not been for the ancients, irreligious Caucasian-Zionism could not have exploited usury throughout the ends of the earth. But they did and have broken all legal limits surrounding the very nature of lending. As a consequence, their economic stability is suffering a painful retribution, never to recover its global toehold. You ask why, because that was not foretold.

---

[25] www.ansarfinance.com/UsuryReligion.asp#HinduismBuddhism

Chapter VI

U.S. Is A Welfare State

The Nation of Islam (NOI) has publicly stated that their founder Wallace Fard Muhammad met with President Herbert Hoover and his staff in 1930. Furthermore, the NOI proclaims his coming to America was in fulfillment to Matthew 24:27 foretold, "*For as lightning that comes from the east is visible even in the west, so will be the coming of the Son of Man. Wherever there is a carcass, there the vultures (birds of prey) will gather.*"

According to Islamic scholar, Tynetta Muhammad, America's Masonic Order (white Moslems), during the turn of the century, was expecting the appearance of such a Divine Person from the east to one-day visit the west for its crimes against Black African slaves. She wrote in her column of the Final Call Newspaper, "The Great Seal of the United States Government uses the image of a truncated pyramid with a missing capstone. In the open space above the pyramid there is placed the symbol of an eye radiating with rays of light. There are 13 course stones that lead up to the missing capstone over which is the All-Eye Seeing.

"Master Fard Muhammad made his appearance on the fourth of July, in the year 1930. July the fourth contains 13 letters. The resolution of the numbers in the date 1930 equals 13. He met with President Herbert Hoover, a name which contains 13 letters. The White House contains 13 letters. The Great Pyramid in Egypt lies on a base of 13 acres.

"A replica of the Great Seal can also be viewed in the George Washington Masonic [MOSLEM SONS] National Monument. The project to construct the Masonic Memorial was initiated on February 22, 1910 and was completed and dedicated on May 12, 1932. This event was attended by President Hoover and his wife and several members of his Cabinet including a long list of Government Dignitaries. This period of time from the inception to the conclusion of the building and dedication of the Washington Memorial covers the twenty-year period in which the Master [W. Fard Muhammad] traveled back and forth to America and met with President Herbert Hoover in 1930."

History informs us Hoover was not your average President. His *"crowd out"*[26]

---

[26] In economics, **crowding out** is any reduction in private consumption or investment that occurs because of an increase in government spending.

economic ideas were indeed sound. It was also his ideas that brought the "*beast*" against his administration from 1930 to 1933. To begin with, Hoover first signed the Smoot-Hawley Tariff Act to form a much larger part of government revenue on over 20,000 dutiable items, despite the protests of economists. Afterward, the bank cartel apparatus immediately retaliated.

> "*Also, between 1930-1932, some 5,100 banks alone in those two years failed as panicked depositors withdrew their funds. Those losses amounted to $3.2 billion. These are considered by some to be* ***Hoover's biggest political blunders (although Hoover himself, years later, said that he felt his only real mistake was to not immediately repudiate the foreign debt, which would have relieved the financial burden on much of Europe early on during the worldwide economic crisis, and thus spurred more trade with the United States).*** *Moreover, the Federal Reserve System's tightening of the money supply (for fear of inflation) is regarded by Milton Friedman and most modern economists as a mistaken strategy, given the situation.*"[27]

To make matters worst Hoover signed the Revenue Act of 1932 (June 6, 1932, ch. 209, 47 Stat. 169) to raise United

[27] http://www.squidoo.com/herbert-hoover

States tax rates across the board, with the rate on top incomes rising from 25 percent to 63 percent. Additionally, estate taxes were doubled and corporate taxes were raised by almost 15 percent. Basically, in 1932, he began increasing taxation on the wealthy and all subsequent taxable years. For this reason, in 1933, Mr. Hoover was jettisoned from office due to retaliation against his policies to prevent a U.S. welfare state establishment under his term.

> *"The provision of* ***a welfare state****, with cradle to grave "security" regardless of the productiveness of those made "secure", is not financed through taxation. What* ***is, partially, financed through taxation is the gigantic bureaucracy necessary to administer such a state. The actual provision of "security" is made, in its entirety, through borrowing, facilitated through the operations of Central Banks and national Treasuries or Ministries of Finance.*** *The original (and only valid) definition of inflation is an increase in the stock of money. Only comparatively recently has the definition come to be a rise in the general price level. The reason for the change in definition is obvious, it conceals the mechanism through which the welfare state is maintained."*[28]

As you can imagine, Hoover's presidency was in jeopardy. His reluctance to implement the Federal Reserve System's provisions to make America a welfare state

---

[28] http://www.usagold.com/gildedopinion/buckler.html

sooner rather than later earned him the raft of those who ultimately went on to conquer America's sovereignty.

President Franklin Roosevelt

President Hoover's administration was replaced by President Franklin D. Roosevelt's administration in 1933. Under the Roosevelt, administration surfaced *The New Deal*. With this deal, all U.S. citizens, in 1936, were required to receive a number (mark of the beast). This era legalized the social security number system (SSN) and it became a law under Federal Reserve Provisions. Each SSN represented income tax dollars needed to finance a gigantic bureaucracy.

Like or not, taxation is necessary to administer a welfare state such as the one we have in the US of A. To resolve this matter, from 1936 onward, U.S. citizens with SSN's became registered assets of the Federal Reserve privatized central bank apparatus.

Sample Social Security Card

Naturally, most people are clueless to what part of prophecy was fulfilled with the onslaught of the New Deal during the

1930's. From its inception, the Social Security Administration was a part of *The New Deal Social Security Program* wherein 25 million numbers were issued to U.S. citizens. Seventy-seven years later, 2010, all who want to own property, gain employment, or buy and sell goods and services must receive a mark—SSN. I think it is safe to say: THE BANK WARS OF THE WESTERN WORLD IS BETWEEN WHITE MOSLEM SONS AND THE SYNAGOGUE OF SATAN.

When the New Deal was signed, sealed and delivered the Bible book of Revelations 14:15-17 was fulfilled by these words, "*He was given power to give breath to the image of the first beast, so that it could speak and cause all who refused to worship the image to be killed. He also forced everyone, small and great, rich and poor, free and slave, to receive a mark on his right hand or on his forehead, so that no one could buy or sell unless he had the mark, which is the name of the beast or the number of his name.*" (See appendix 1, Commercial Nations of the SSN, National ID and/or National Insurance Card system)

The United States of America has the best social systems of any nation on earth. Her main downside is the nature of "its" monetary policy designed to prey upon U.S. tax dollars.

In terms of Black America's struggle toward economic freedom, the destruction our pride and joy called *Black* Wall Street in 1921, Tulsa Oklahama demonstrated how the wicked in high places really fought to keep the former slaves under a Master/slave relationship more than any other ethnic group inside of America. And although *Black* Wall Street was economically destroyed[29] by local Christian militiamen and others, including state government "officials, America's economic sovereignty was likewise destroyed in 1933 by international bankers with *The New Deal.*

"The Great Depression had devastated the nation by the time Roosevelt took office in 1933. Every bank in the nation had closed its doors and no one could cash a check or get at their savings. The unemployment rate was 25% and higher in major industrial and mining centers. Farm prices had fallen by 50%. Thousands of mortgages closed down..

"The New Deal represented a significant shift in political and domestic policy in the U.S., its more

[29] This hidden part of history is fully exposed on www.blackwallstreet.freeservers.com. Learn how over 15,000 Black people were left homeless, then run out of town and thousands were killed or wounded by fellow white Americans on May 31st, and June 1st in 1921. [source: www.blackwallstreet.freeservers.com/]

lasting changes being increased federal government control over the economy and money supply, intervention to control prices and agricultural production. It also marked the beginning of complex social programs and growing power of labor unions. The effects of the New Deal still remain a source of controversy and debate amongst economists and historians."[30]

President Franklin D. Roosevelt coined the name, *New Deal*, for his complex package of economic programs from 1933-36. His agenda was to generate 1) **Relief** to the unemployed and badly hurt farmers, 2) **Reform** of business and financial practices, and 3) **Recovery** of the economy during the Great Depression. During Roosevelt's initial meetings to ease problems, he dealt with groups of bankers, farmers and railroad magnets and industry builders. If this reminds you of President Obama's actions don't be surprised. It will be shown to you in the final chapter how and why this world's best minds only have access to 33 degrees of knowledge.

Imagine, if you will, a need for liquid water to put out a fire but the weather will only generate a 33 degree *Fahrenheit*

[30] http://en.wikipedia.org/wiki/New_Deal

temperature. Under these conditions, water is just above a freeze, hardly melting.

Boom And Bust Economics

The unemployment chart below demonstrates the temporary upshot of Franklin D. Roosevelt's New Deal boom and bust economics. What you see on the chart from year 1933 – 1945 is stimulus from usury fiat-money or inflation/deflation economics.

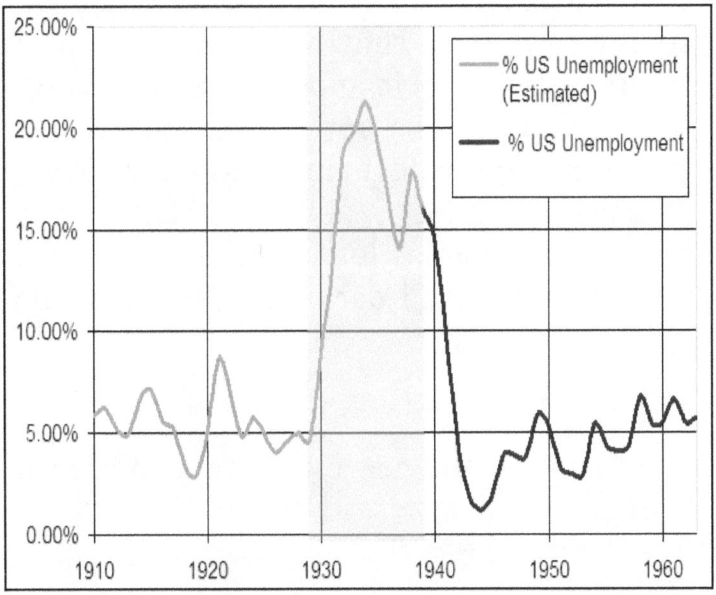

All western world economies are modeled after boom and bust, a type of cycle experienced by an economy characterized by alternating periods of economic growth and contraction. During booms, an economy based on inflation, you will see an increase in its production and Gross Domestic Product's (GDP) national and international sells. During busts cycles (deflation), the economy falls in production and unemployment increases because national or international products are not being produced nor sold.

The irony here is America's doctors of law, government officials, political leaders, military scientists and financial wizards changed every monetary rule imagined simply to prevent third-world nations from competing in their global market. Their world view was so anti-Christ that they'd rather employ debt finance rooted in usury, which weighed down their own government, just as long as it also hindered the rise of original dark skin people of the earth.

Who Stole The Gold

One of the gravest secrets American historians do not often mention is how Gold certificates were used as paper currency and freely convertible into gold coins. Furthermore,

Sample $100 gold certificate

historians do not publicly mention why U.S. gold certificates were suspended.

It happened because Europe's central bank of England was gold-broke and had been so since 1914. Subsequently, faced with the need to fund high levels of expenditure (spending) to maintain an incestrious global empire of murder and mayhem between Europe's royal courts, it was necessary to pimp the new world economy. To make this scheme succeed globally, America needed to suspend her gold standard system too..

Thus, under the 1933 Presidential Executive Order of Franklin D. Roosevelt, on April 5, 1933 U.S. gold was confiscated and/or stolen; under the color of law, from U.S. citizens to allow international bankers experimental Principle Of *Elasticity* Of *Money* to expand and open new commercial markets throughout the earth. Thereafter, a flood of Federal Reserves Notes or fiat money expanded its way through a fractional reserve bank system creating a windfall of profits for Central Banks from the U.S. to England. By 1974, the entire world was pegged with using the U.S. dollar.

Did American citizens agree giving their gold coins over to the Federal government? No! Of course, anyone refusing to follow the '33 Executive Order was threatened with a $10,000 fine or 10-year prison sentence. Part of the New Deal required everyone to exchange their gold coin certificates for newly issued Federal Reserve Notes. President Roosevelt rationalized his usurpation of private property rights on gold in one of his famous fireside chats. "*Since there was not enough gold to pay all holders of gold obligations,*" he claimed, "*the Government should in the interest of justice allow none to be paid in gold.*"[31] See original executive order announcement on the following page.

> "*After the gold was received, the government melted the majority of the coins. The government then raised gold's value by nearly 75%.* ***These government actions helped President Roosevelt and Congress inflate the U.S. economy during the mid- and late-1930s. These actions also led to a loss of a number of important freedoms for the American people - freedoms from long-term inflation, expanding government, gold confiscation (except collectors),*** *and government intrusion into their private financial matters.*"[32]

[31] www.independent.org/publications/article.asp?id=165
[32] http://www.wellsfargonevadagold.com/exec-order.html

POSTMASTER: PLEASE POST IN A CONSPICUOUS PLACE.—JAMES A. FARLEY, Postmaster General

UNDER EXECUTIVE ORDER OF THE PRESIDENT

Issued April 5, 1933

all persons are required to deliver

ON OR BEFORE MAY 1, 1933

all GOLD COIN, GOLD BULLION, AND GOLD CERTIFICATES now owned by them to a Federal Reserve Bank, branch or agency, or to any member bank of the Federal Reserve System.

Executive Order

FORBIDDING THE HOARDING OF GOLD COIN, GOLD BULLION AND GOLD CERTIFICATES.

By virtue of the authority vested in me by Section 5(b) of the Act of October 6, 1917, as amended by Section 2 of the Act of March 9, 1933, entitled "An Act to provide relief in the existing national emergency in banking, and for other purposes", in which amendatory Act Congress declared that a serious emergency exists, I, Franklin D. Roosevelt, President of the United States of America, do declare that said national emergency still continues to exist and pursuant to said section do hereby prohibit the hoarding of gold coin, gold bullion, and gold certificates within the continental United States by individuals, partnerships, associations and corporations and hereby prescribe the following regulations for carrying out the purposes of this order:

Section 1. For the purposes of this regulation, the term "hoarding" means the withdrawal and withholding of gold coin, gold bullion or gold certificates from the recognized and customary channels of trade. The term "person" means any individual, partnership, association or corporation.

Section 2. All persons are hereby required to deliver on or before May 1, 1933, to a Federal reserve bank or a branch or agency thereof or to any member bank of the Federal Reserve System all gold coin, gold bullion and gold certificates now owned by them or coming into their ownership on or before April 28, 1933, except the following:

(a) Such amount of gold as may be required for legitimate and customary use in industry, profession or art within a reasonable time, including gold prior to refining and stocks of gold in reasonable amounts for the usual trade requirements of owners mining and refining such gold.

(b) Gold coin and gold certificates in an amount not exceeding in the aggregate $100.00 belonging to any one person; and gold coins having a recognized special value to collectors of rare and unusual coins.

(c) Gold coin and bullion earmarked or held in trust for a recognized foreign government or foreign central bank or the Bank for International Settlements.

(d) Gold coin and bullion licensed for other proper transactions (not involving hoarding) including gold coin and bullion imported for reexport or held pending action on applications for export licenses.

Section 3. Until otherwise ordered any person becoming the owner of any gold coin, gold bullion, or gold certificates after April 28, 1933, shall, within three days after receipt thereof, deliver the same in the manner prescribed in Section 2; unless such gold coin, gold bullion or gold certificates are held for any of the purposes specified in paragraphs (a), (b) or (c) of Section 2; or unless such gold coin or gold bullion is held for purposes specified in paragraph (d) of Section 2 and the person holding it is, with respect to such gold coin or bullion, a licensee or applicant for license pending action thereon.

Section 4. Upon receipt of gold coin, gold bullion or gold certificates delivered to it in accordance with Sections 2 or 3, the Federal reserve bank or member bank will pay therefor an equivalent amount of any other form of coin or currency coined or issued under the laws of the United States.

Section 5. Member banks shall deliver all gold coin, gold bullion and gold certificates owned or received by them (other than as exempted under the provisions of Section 2) to the Federal reserve banks of their respective districts and receive credit or payment therefor.

Section 6. The Secretary of the Treasury, out of the sum made available to the President by Section 501 of the Act of March 9, 1933, will in all proper cases pay the reasonable costs of transportation of gold coin, gold bullion or gold certificates delivered to a member bank or Federal reserve bank in accordance with Sections 2, 3, or 5 hereof, including the cost of insurance, protection, and such other incidental costs as may be necessary, upon production of satisfactory evidence of such costs. Voucher forms for this purpose may be procured from Federal reserve banks.

Section 7. In cases where the delivery of gold coin, gold bullion or gold certificates by the owners thereof within the time set forth above will involve extraordinary hardship or difficulty, the Secretary of the Treasury may, in his discretion, extend the time within which such delivery must be made. Applications for such extensions must be made in writing under oath, addressed to the Secretary of the Treasury and filed with a Federal reserve bank. Each application must state the date to which the extension is desired, the amount and location of the gold coin, gold bullion and gold certificates in respect of which such application is made and the facts showing extension to be necessary to avoid extraordinary hardship or difficulty.

Section 8. The Secretary of the Treasury is hereby authorized and empowered to issue such further regulations as he may deem necessary to carry out the purposes of this order and to issue licenses thereunder, through such officers or agencies as he may designate, including licenses permitting the Federal reserve banks and member banks of the Federal Reserve System, in return for an equivalent amount of other coin, currency or credit, to deliver, earmark or hold in trust gold coin and bullion to or for persons showing the need for the same for any of the purposes specified in paragraphs (a), (c) and (d) of Section 2 of these regulations.

Section 9. Whoever willfully violates any provision of this Executive Order or of these regulations or of any rule, regulation or license issued thereunder may be fined not more than $10,000, or, if a natural person, may be imprisoned for not more than ten years, or both; and any officer, director, or agent of any corporation who knowingly participates in any such violation may be punished by a like fine, imprisonment, or both.

This order and these regulations may be modified or revoked at any time.

THE WHITE HOUSE
April 5, 1933.

FRANKLIN D ROOSEVELT

For Further Information Consult Your Local Bank

GOLD CERTIFICATES may be identified by the words "GOLD CERTIFICATE" appearing thereon. The serial number and the Treasury seal on the face of a GOLD CERTIFICATE are printed in YELLOW. Be careful not to confuse GOLD CERTIFICATES with other issues which are redeemable in gold but which are not GOLD CERTIFICATES. Federal Reserve Notes and United States Notes are "redeemable in gold" but are not "GOLD CERTIFICATES" and are not required to be surrendered

Special attention is directed to the exceptions allowed under Section 2 of the Executive Order

CRIMINAL PENALTIES FOR VIOLATION OF EXECUTIVE ORDER $10,000 fine or 10 years imprisonment, or both, as provided in Section 9 of the order

W. H. Woodin
Secretary of the Treasury.

U.S. Government Printing Office: 1933 2-16064

Japan Loses Gold War

A brief study of 16th century Japan will substantiate how Europe tricked them out of their gold.

"From 1601, the Tokugawa coinage consisted in gold, silver, and bronze denominations. In 1858, Western countries, especially the United States, France and Great Britain imposed through "unequal treaties" (Treaty of Amity and Commerce) free trade, free monetary flow, and very low tariffs, effectively taking away Japanese control of its foreign exchange. The 1715 export embargo on gold bullion was thus lifted:
"All foreign coin shall be current in Japan and pass for its corresponding weight of Japanese coin of the same description... Coins of all description (with the exception of Japanese copper coin) may be exported from Japan" — Treaty of Amity and Commerce, 1858.

"This created a massive outflow of gold from Japan, as foreigners rushed to exchange their silver for "token" silver Japanese coinage and again exchange these against gold, giving a 200% profit to the transaction. In 1860, about 70 tons of gold thus left Japan, effectively destroying Japan's gold standard system, and forced it to return to weight-based system with international rates. The Bakufu responded to the crises by debasing the gold content of its coins by two thirds, so as to match foreign gold-silver exchange ratios.

"As a consequence, the Tokugawa Bakufu lost the major profit source of recoinage (seniorage), and was forced to issue unbacked paper money, leading to major inflation. This was one of the major causes of discontent during the

Bakumatsu period, and one of the causes of the demise of the Shogunate.[33]

After Japan lost its right to value their own currency, the people were forced to act according to Satan's global monetary policy. As you can see, a pile of tricks exercised at its best against Japan for the sake of a boom and bust economic world order.

In 2010, going forward, no more western tricks can hatch against third-world nations, except maybe file for global bankruptcy. Between the technological advances, economic wherewithal and market-wise far easterners, Europe and America will never return to its former world power status.

China, Singapore, Japan—Asian nations in general retain almost 50% of U.S. government bonds and/or tonnes of gold bullion purchased from America, France and other European central banks. As the old adage says, tick-tock the game is locked.

China & Japan Will Unite

On August 21, 1968 the leader of the Nation of Islam, Elijah Muhammad stated, "China [and], Russia [they] just nervous to

[33] http://en.wikipedia.org/wiki/Gold_standard

get at them. Japan will come out with China when she sees the U.S. power weaken.[34]

The chart below gives one a better picture of U.S. deficit spending from 2006 to 2009.

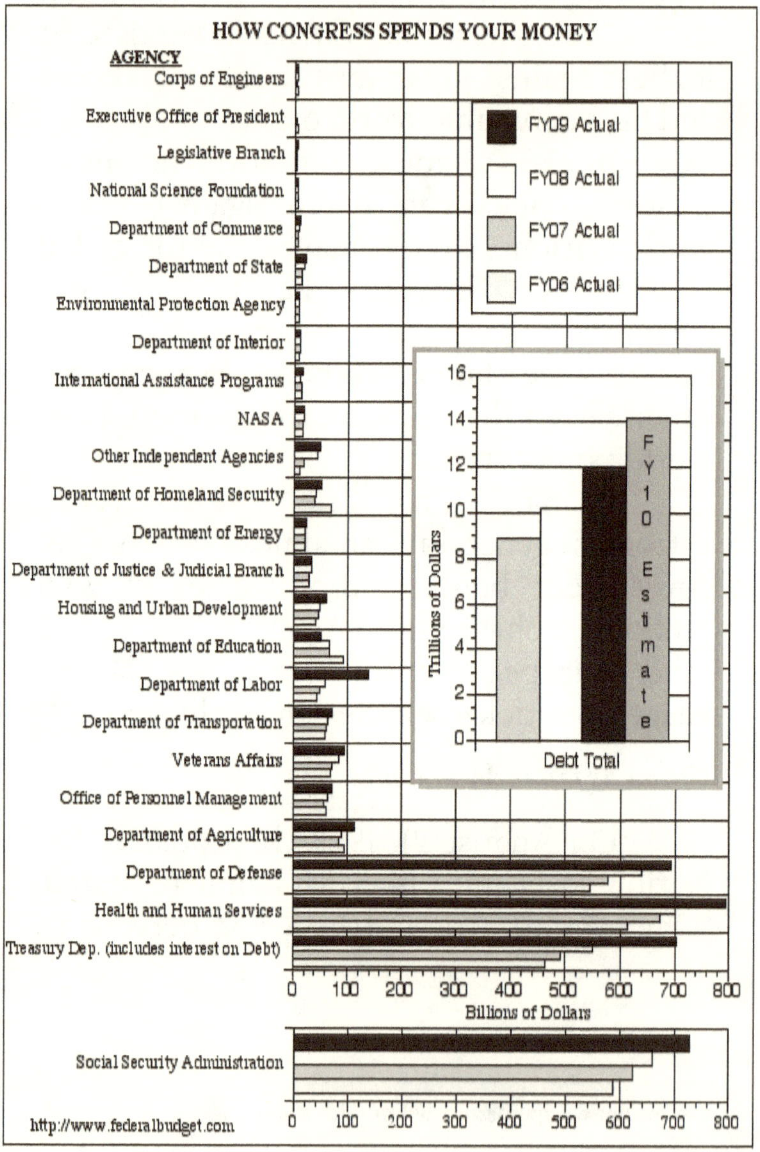

Unfortunately, the primary product or asset being pawned to the world by the U.S. federal government to help pay down its national debt is U.S. income taxes, sales taxes and other taxes in general.

The formula to tally total deficits is spending plus interest payments on the debt minus tax revenues (Spending + Interest − tax Revenues = total deficit). Altogether, the U.S. Federal deficit equals 14 trillion dollars and mounting. The lack of national revenue production, jobs and more borrowing and gold debasement; of course, make U.S. dollars a faulty piece of paper in which bondholders rely upon to earn usury profits for their investment in the U.S. economy. Despite job losses, "*we the people*" are being propped up as a gross domestic product (GDP) or asset to justify more government borrowing and selling of rentes (a government security bond that pays interest).

In an indistinguishable cruel way, American labor is a collateral, by which central banks will lend, in the place wherein gold once upon a time collateralized lending. Lo and behold, the undoing of the white mans world began in 1914.

"Since the US Federal Reserve was formed in 1913, however, the US dollar has fallen to barely a

twentieth of its former value through the consistently inflationary policies of the bank. Economists counter that deflation is hard to control once it sets in and its effects are much more damaging than modest, consistent inflation.

"Ultimately, banks or governments relying heavily on seigniorage and fractional reserve sources of revenue will find it counterproductive.

Rational expectations of inflation take into account a bank's seigniorage strategy, leading to economy-damaging hyperinflation.

Instead of accruing seigniorage from fiat money and credit most governments opt to raise revenue primarily through taxation and other means.[35]

Original U.S. Constitution

What is Seigniorage? Seiniorage is derived from specie—**metal coins i.e., gold/silver**—arises from the difference between the face value of a coin and the cost of producing, distributing and retiring it from circulation. Knowing when to retire worn out issued currency from circulation is one key to renewing the wealth of a society and its central government operations based upon an honest money supply.

---

[35] http://en.wikipedia.org/wiki/Federal_Reserve_System]

On the other hand, Seigniorage derived from notes (paper money) is more indirect, being the difference between interests earned on securities acquired in exchange for bank notes and the costs of producing and distributing those notes. Under these terms, Seigniorage is regarded as a form of inflation tax, as paying for government services by issuing new currency with the effect of creating a de facto tax that falls on those who hold the existing currency. In the U.S., "we the people" hold the existing currency resulting in its effective devaluation through the introduction of additional money printed at the whim of the Federal Government. That's why, the worldwide debt is valued at 100 trillion dollars. America's misunderstanding of true Seigniorage and ravenousness has led to her ruin.

The constitution of the United States was originally intended to prevent America's financial disaster. In part, it states: Art. I Sec. 8 Cl. 5 stated: [Congress shall have Power...] To coin Money, regulate the Value thereof, and of foreign Coin, ...; Art. I Sec. 10 Cl. 1 [No State shall ...] make any Thing but gold and silver Coin a Tender in Payment of Debts; ...

Note that there is no such prohibition against Congress, or any delegated power to make anything-legal tender. Congress was originally understood to have no power to make anything-legal tender outside of federal territories, under Art. I Sec. 8 Cl. 17 and Art. IV Sec. 3 Cl. 2, but in 1868 a Supreme Court packed by Pres. Ulysses S. Grant, in the *Legal Tender Cases*, allowed Congress to make paper currency issued by the U.S. Treasury, backed by gold, legal tender on state territory, a precedent that remains controversial to this day, when courts allow paper currency not backed by anything to be considered "legal tender".[36]

Was it misunderstanding about true Seigniorage that led to America finanical ruin? Alternatively, was greed and eagerness for a modern world built upon concrete, electricity and steel? Whatever the case may be, it appears U.S. leaders—so-called best minds—could not and still cannot design a productive honest money system to free its citizens from debt and bondage from the Synagogue of Satan.

Greed and eagerness has and is destroying both the Jews and Gentiles world order. Their limited knowledge about currency is evident. Their best minds do not have the discipline or nature to administer

---

[36] http://www.constitution.org/cs_money.htm

financial instruments and wealth of the earth for six billion people.

In summary, the entire Western world are victims of their own covet behavior, which was a subject that prophet Moses and Jesus warned them against thousands of years ago.

Chapter VII

Allah Is Not Against Money

God is not against money. God and the righteous are in opposition against excess usury. When usury is employed a government and its people, under such plague, are ruined over time. Of course, excess usury may be a quick fix to get rich for central bankers and loan sharks, but eventually, it destroys the true wealth of any nation.

Take for instance commercial credit. This form of usury is the principal medium by means of which trade exchanges are carried on in the distribution of goods. The entire industrial organization of today is based upon usury credit access.

Our process of distributing goods from the grower or original producer to the ultimate consumer involves the services of many middlemen manufacturers, brokers, wholesalers, jobbers, importers and retailers who must all borrow from bank cartels to get their business off the ground. Each of these in turn frequently has to buy goods on usury credit. A few business concerns are so situated that they can always pay cash. Ninety percent, however, need credit. The farmer or planter goes into debt for his seed, fertilizer and machinery agreeing to make payments when his crop is sold; the manufacturer purchases his raw materials with debt finance and sells his manufactured product to the wholesaler who is debt financed. And so on through the whole chain of distribution. You want to know why prices are getting sky-high, because the *devils [usury fee] is in the details.*

Every business must borrow or get credit with interest. The interest rate is then added to the cost of their goods in the retail price that consumers buy at the market place. So, by the time each product reaches us (consumer), our purchase power is destabilized. We are paying multiple sums of usurious interest rates tagged onto goods and services. Excess usurious interest rates are hidden in the cost of all productivity, including "In God We Trust."

"*A central bank, reserve bank, or monetary authority is a banking institution granted the exclusive privilege to lend a government its currency. Like a normal commercial bank, a central bank charges interest on the loans made to borrowers, primarily the government of whichever country the bank exists for, and to other commercial banks, typically as a 'lender of last resort'. However, a central bank is distinguished from a normal commercial bank because it has a monopoly on creating the currency of that nation, which is loaned to the government in the form of legal tender.*

It is a bank that can lend money to other banks in times of need. Its primary function is to provide the nation's money supply, but more active duties include controlling subsidized-loan interest rates, and acting as a lender of last resort to the banking sector during times of financial crisis (private banks often being integral to the national financial system). It may also have supervisory powers, to ensure that banks and other financial institutions do not behave recklessly or fraudulently.

"***Most richer countries today have an 'independent" central bank, that is, one which operates under rules designed to prevent political interference. Examples include the European Central Bank (ECB) and the Federal Reserve System in the United States.*** *Some central banks are publicly owned, and others are privately owned. For example, the United States Federal Reserve is a quasi-public corporation.*"[37]

Ancient Islamic and Jewish Economics

After the classical Islamic and orthodox Jewish world's capitalism and free markets were made subject to satanic leadership centuries ago, a more corrupt version of banking and economic practices came into power. By this I mean, several

[37] http://en.wikipedia.org/wiki/IMF

unholy alliances between the western Roman Catholic Papacy, Christian nobles and kings and Talmudic Jewish merchants of the 13th, 14th, 15th and 16th century were predisposed to exalt Anglo genetic and intellectual endogamous superiority.

Even though 13th and 14th century Europeans borrowed many superior ideas from the Islamic and orthodox Jewish world, they where not able to fully exploit the knowledge until after 1492.

"The origins of capitalism and free markets can be traced back to the Islamic Golden Age and Muslim Agricultural Revolution, where the first market economy and earliest forms of merchant capitalism took root between the 8th–12th centuries, which some refer to as "Islamic capitalism". A vigorous monetary economy was created by Muslims on the basis of the expanding levels of circulation of a stable high-value currency (the dinar) and the integration of monetary areas that were previously independent. Innovative new business techniques and forms of business organisation were introduced by economists, merchants and traders during this time. Such innovations included the earliest trading companies, big businesses, contracts, bills of exchange, long-distance international trade, the first forms of partnership (mufawada) such as

limited partnerships (mudaraba), and the earliest forms of credit, debt, profit, loss, capital (al-mal), capital accumulation (nama al-mal), circulating capital, capital expenditure, revenue, cheques, promissory notes, trusts (see Waqf), startup companies, savings accounts, transactional accounts, pawning, loaning, exchange rates, bankers, money changers, ledgers, deposits, assignments, the double-entry bookkeeping system, and lawsuits. Organizational enterprises similar to corporations independent from the state also existed in the medieval Islamic world, while the agency institution was also introduced. Many of these early capitalist concepts were adopted and further advanced in medieval Europe from the 13th century onwards.

"The systems of contract relied upon by merchants was very effective. Merchants would buy and sell on commission, with money loaned to them by wealthy investors, or a joint investment of several merchants, who were often Muslim, Christian and Jewish. Recently, a collection of documents was found in an Egyptian synagogue shedding a very detailed and human light on the life of medieval Middle Eastern merchants. Business partnerships would be made for many commercial ventures, and bonds of kinship enabled trade networks to form over huge

distances. Networks developed during this time enabled a world in which money could be promised by a bank in Baghdad and cashed in Spain, creating the cheque system of today. Each time items passed through the cities along this extraordinary network, the city imposed a tax, resulting in high prices once reaching the final destination. These innovations made by Muslims and Jews laid the foundations for the modern economic system.[38]

So-called third world nations are poised to take their rightful place on the global scene. As it was in the beginning, so shall it be in the ending is not just a religious slogan. Black America in particular has one the most important roles to fulfill of any so-called third world people.

Your Federal Reserve System

Some would argue without the Federal Reserve System, the landscape and energy consumed by America would have malfunctioned long ago especially after the 1929 great depression. In other words, where it not for the Federal Reserve System, America and Europe's sway over the other nations would have been invalid. So in exchange for unlimited access to Europe's

[38] http://en.wikipedia.org/wiki/Islamic_capitalism

bank cartel fiat money, America's market-wise officially joined the cartel. Her political figureheads only needed to perform a feoffment (fiefdom) or *livery of seisin*, which is a ceremony for transferring the possession of real property from one person to another. Except in our case, the real property transferred was U.S. citizenry, including white folks. The person or entity to which "*we the people*" were transferred is none other than the Federal Reserve Privatized Bank System. To this private entity, every living man, women and child are a source of tax revenue.

The *livery of seisin* commenced in 1913 at the U.S. House of Congress. It was performed practically in secret but its words were recorded and written into law as follows:

<u>Federal Reserve Act December 23, 1913</u>

"An Act To provide for the establishment of Federal reserve banks, to furnish an elastic currency, to afford means of rediscounting commercial paper, to establish a more effective supervision of banking in the United States, and for other purposes...

"Under regulations to be prescribed by the organization committee, every national banking association in the United States is hereby required, and every eligible bank in the United States and every trust company within the District of Columbia, is hereby authorized to signify in

writing, within sixty days after the passage of this Act, its acceptance of the terms and provisions hereof...

"SEC. 25. Any national banking association possessing a capital and surplus of $ 1,000, 000 or more may file application with the Federal Reserve Board . . . for the purpose of securing authority to establish branches in foreign countries or dependencies of the United States for the furtherance of the foreign commerce of the United States, and to act, if required to do so, as fiscal agents of the United States.... The Federal Reserve Board shall have power to approve or to reject such application if, in its judgment, the amount of capital proposed to be set aside for the conduct of foreign business is inadequate, or if for other reasons the granting of such application is deemed inexpedient... Approved, December 23, 1913,..."[39]

A key agenda of the Federal Reserve Act agreement was designed to enable America's newly formed private central bank to print and loan fiat money almost risk free to the U.S. government as long as U.S. land and taxpayers (citizens) serve as the necessary collateral (Surety) to guarantee repayment. I reiterate, under these terms, a *livery of seisin* was performed in 1913. Not in old Europe, but in America.

Whether you agreed or disagreed with the *livery of seisin*, everyone was transferred to a new owner[s] i.e. the stockholders of the Federal Reserve Banking

[39] www.historycentral.com/documents/Federalreserve.html

System. Whether you like it or not, as long as "*we the people*" are working, paying income and sales taxes, "we" represent a guarantee that the international banks and financial cartels will make a profit for printing, lending and investing into the U.S. economy.

When the Federal Reserve Act of 1913 was signed, sealed and delivered Europe's Bank cartels (that also had adopted several U.S. banking families) were guaranteed that the interest rate at which they lent money to the U.S. Government would be collected in the name of federal income taxes. This agreement was not made for the glory of God, but was instead dedicated to the glory of the ruling class of the Caucasian race. Of course, today Asia owns a great deal now and the Buddhist will not give up its gaining power and advantage.

33 Degrees of Knowledge

The rulers of today's socio-economic, political and religious order only have access to 33 degrees of God's Knowledge into the true meaning of civilization and divine life itself. Officially sanctioned war crimes, poverty policies, criminal acts, licentious entertainment, betrayal, feelings of rancor and host of other ills of mans uncontrollable thoughts evince how low ones mind can devolve. Ones action determines his or her degree of knowledge.

Any mathematician knows that **MAN** needs a least 90 degrees of know how to at least stand perpendicular—**upright** to the plane of the ecliptic.

Diagram 1 on the next page demonstrates the difference between upright behavior and beast-like behavior or worse. If mans mind is ill formed, handicapped and misguided, his actions will reflect the actions of a beast in human form i.e., 33 degrees.

Diagram 1

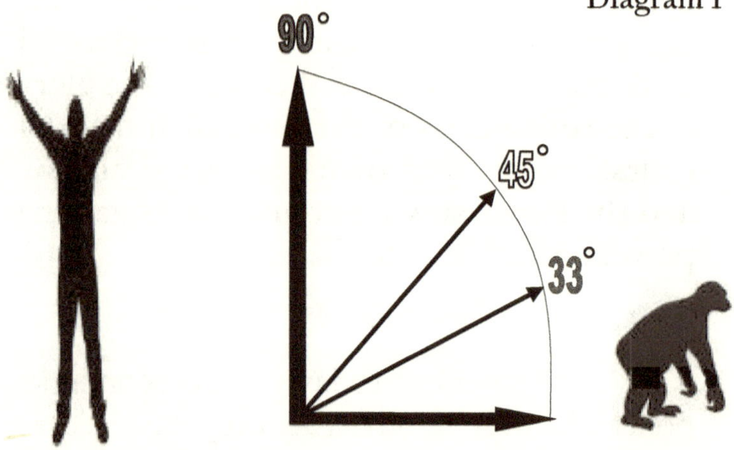

With 33 degrees or less, you see man is barely standing. With 90 degrees man can stand upright to live upon principles of honorable conductivity. To the low-life, honorable conduct is a joke and a weakness. My point is that the mentality of Europe's so-called elite is powereed by 33°s of knowledge under which all nations have been subdued by the hand of death and mischief.

Before the fall of the first people on earth {Genesis 3}, civilization was upright—men and women were righteous. Heaven was established on earth in the east. After the fall, however, civilization's modem was downgraded and the Supreme Knowledge of God and the Science of everything in life was gradually withdrawn. Mankind's mentality became malnourished with only 33 degrees of knowledge. Genesis 3:3 reads, *"But of the fruit of the tree which [is] in the midst of the garden, God hath said, Ye shall not eat of it, neither shall ye touch it, lest ye die."* Experimenting with and grafting from divine knowledge to make mischief has lead to the poisons of death.

Before the spiritual and emotional fall of humanity, living Gods law was important and foremost to people. After the fall, that importance was reduced. Today talking God's law has taken precedence over doing and living the way God intended in science and peace and not merely for sport and play although sport and play has its place.

White mankind was ultimately put over fallen civilization and the currency belonging to it. Consequently, their best and brightest minds (including those under western scholarship, education, tutelage and culture) at present think with limited justness.

For that reason, the scriptures have always foretold about a new man who is yet to come and to bring a New Knowledge. I suggest you read "*FARRAKHAN The Jesus Factor*" for more understanding about the new man and new world to come after the fall of the beast and its outdated Master/slave idealogy. (*Revelation* 2:9; 3:9)

Appendix 1

- 1 Argentina
- 2 Australia
- 3 Austria
- 4 Belgium
- 5 Brazil
- 6 Bulgaria
- 7 Canada
- 8 Chile
- 9 People's Republic of China
- 10 Colombia
- 11 Croatia
- 12 Czech Republic
- 13 Denmark
- 14 Estonia
- 15 European Economic Area / Switzerland
- 16 Finland
- 17 France
- 18 Greece
- 19 Germany
- 20 Hong Kong
- 21 Hungary
- 22 Iceland
- 23 India (new 2010 policy)
- 24 Indonesia
- 25 Iran, Islamic Republic of
- 26 Ireland
- 27 Israel
- 28 Italy
- 29 Latvia
- 30 Lithuania
- 31 Macau
- 32 Macedonia
- 33 Malaysia
- 34 Mexico
- 35 Montenegro
- 36 Netherlands
- 37 New Zealand
- 38 Norway
- 39 Pakistan
- 40 Poland
- 41 Portugal
- 42 Romania
- 43 San Marino
- 44 Singapore
- 45 Slovakia
- 46 Slovenia
- 47 South Africa
- 48 South Korea
- 49 Spain
- 50 Sri Lanka
- 51 Sweden
- 52 Switzerland
- 53 Republic of China (Taiwan)
- 54 Thailand
- 55 Turkey
- 56 Ukraine
- 57 United Kingdom
- 58 United States
- 59 Former Yugoslav republics

On Sale Now

noidecoded@yahoo.com for questions

www.ingramcontent.com/pod-product-compliance
Lightning Source LLC
Chambersburg PA
CBHW022057170526
45157CB00004B/1385
* 9 7 8 1 4 5 3 6 9 6 3 0 9 *